FUN IN

INCLUDING RENO & LAKE TAHOE 1988

1988

Stephen Allen
Connie Emerson

FODOR'S TRAVEL PUBLICATIONS, INC.
New York & London

ISBN 0–679–01508–6
ISBN 0–340–42491–5   (Hodder & Stoughton)

Maps and plans by Burmar Technical Corp., Mark Stein Studios
Illustrations by Ted Burwell, Steve Cook, Michael Kaplan

New titles in the series

Barbados

Jamaica

also available

Acapulco

Bahamas

Disney World & the Orlando Area

London

Maui

Montreal

New Orleans

New York City

Paris

Rio

St. Martin/St. Maarten

San Francisco

Waikiki

MANUFACTURED IN THE UNITED STATES OF AMERICA
10 9 8 7 6 5 4 3 2 1

Contents

MAPS AND PLANS

EDITOR'S NOTE

While every care has been taken to ensure the accuracy of the information contained in this guide, the publishers cannot accept responsibility for any errors that may appear.

All prices quoted in this guide are based on those available to us at the time of writing. In a world of rapid change, however, the possibility of inaccurate or out-of-date information can never be totally eliminated. We trust, therefore, that you will take prices quoted as indicators only, and will double-check to be sure of the latest figures. Similarly, be sure to check all opening times of museums and galleries. We have found that such times are liable to change without notice, and you could easily make a trip only to find a locked door. When a hotel closes or a restaurant produces a disappointing meal, let us know, and we will investigate the establishment and the complaint. We are always ready to revise our entries for the following year's edition should the facts warrant it.

Send your letters to the editors of Fodor's Travel Publications, 201 E. 50th Street, New York, NY 10022. Continental or British Commonwealth readers may prefer to write to Fodor's Travel Guides, 9–10 Market Place, London W1N 7AG, England.

Overview

"Las Vegas" does not mean "Lost Wages," as the cynics would have it, but instead means (from the Spanish) "The Meadows"—although you won't find many meadows there now.

What you *will* find is probably the most famous city for its size (less than 500,000 population in the metropolitan area and most of that growth within the past 20 years) in the entire world. And you will find "The Entertainment Capital of the World."

Even most cynics would grudgingly admit that if they had the chance to go to Las Vegas they would. Other people who have come here from the boondocks, and decided to stay, feel they have died and gone to heaven.

Las Vegas *is* an exciting place. If you want nonstop action, Las Vegas has it. If you want the world's only real 24-hour-a-day town, you've got it. If you're the kind of person who never liked to have your parents turn out the lights on you at night, then Las Vegas is your kind of place. No one will ever turn the lights out on you here.

Critics may tell you that many a person arrives in Las Vegas in a $10,000 car and leaves in a $100,000 vehicle: a Greyhound bus. They also say there is a broken wallet for every light in the Great White Way of the fabulous Las Vegas Strip.

But only those people who simply *cannot* control their lust for gambling go away from Las Vegas unhappy. For the rest of us, Las Vegas is a Disneyland for adults, a Sodom in the sand, a Shangri-la in the sun—you get the idea. You can have the time of your life in Las Vegas, while also discovering one of the greatest bargain-vacation destinations in America.

In comparison with other major resort cities around the United States and the rest of the world, you will find that the rates for rooms and meals are low in Las Vegas. There is a reason for this, of course: Gambling pays for part of what you get for your money. Luxury hotel room rates, for instance, are about half what they would be in any other major city.

Hotels such as Caesars Palace and Bally's Las Vegas were not built by sending people home from Las Vegas with more money than they brought, but occasionally it does happen that someone will pop $3 into a progressive dollar slot machine and win $1,000,000. No kidding, it's happened.

But you should assume that you are going to *lose* your gambling money, so set a limit for yourself before you come here—and stick to it. When it's gone, it's gone. There are plenty of other things to do in Las Vegas—as we are about to show you.

The analogy of Las Vegas to an oasis in the desert is not unfounded. "The City that Bugsy Built" (an unfair description) sits in the middle of the desert, about equal distance—300 miles—from Los Angeles and Phoenix. Las Vegas has no reason for being where it is other than to be an entertainment/resort capital, and that's what makes it so delightful: No one expects you to do anything but have a good time.

So let's!

A BRIEF, IRREVERENT HISTORY

Las Vegas is a relatively new city, but it is older than many people think. In 1850, a group of about 30 Mormons from Utah came to the area that is now Las Vegas to build a fort to protect the new Salt Lake City–Los Angeles mail route.

The first settlers tried to farm, but they found that you could not make anything green grow in Las Vegas. (Little did they know.) Then they opened a lead mine at nearby Potosi Mountain, but unfortunately the bullets made from the lead were flaky and brittle (an appellation that is now given to the residents of Las Vegas). Finally, in despair, they gave up and returned to Utah, and Las Vegas was returned to the Indians.

The area remained little more than an oasis in the desert until shortly after the turn of the century, when it became a major stop on the San Pedro, Los Angeles, and Salt Lake Railroad. The railroad acquired the title and water rights to the land around the track, and in an attempt to establish a real town there, it divided the land into 1,200 lots and auctioned them off in 1905. With a population of only 800, the city of Las Vegas was incorporated in 1911.

The Las Vegas area did not really start to grow until 1931, however, when two fortunate things occurred in the same year: In an effort to lift Nevada out of the Depression, the state legislature legalized gambling; and construction was started on Hoover Dam, which is only 30 miles from Las Vegas.

Construction of the dam provided a great deal of money to the people who came to the Las Vegas area, and the legalization of gambling gave them something to do with it. The success and growth of Las Vegas were assured.

But the Las Vegas that you see today really stems from a period shortly after World War II, when the area caught the eye of mobster Benjamin "Bugsy" Siegel. Gambling was legal in Las Vegas, and Las Vegas was the nearest gambling city to Los Angeles. What more could you ask?

Building materials were not easy to come by in the years that followed the war, but Bugsy got 'em somehow and built the lavish Flamingo Hotel, named after his girlfriend, Virginia "Flamingo" Hill. The Flamingo was an idea ahead of its time, and the hotel went bust, but Bugsy had planted a seed that would take root and flourish at a later date. (Bugsy subsequently was killed in Los Angeles in typical gangland fashion.)

The Flamingo Hotel is still in Las Vegas—greatly enlarged and renovated—but now it is called the Flamingo Hilton.

Some people—we won't mention who—think it is a crime that there has never been any monument erected to honor Bugsy in Las Vegas. The only memorial to his name is a little rose garden behind the Flamingo Hilton. A plaque in the garden informs visitors that never did the roses blow so red as just after Bugsy lost a near and dear friend. There is no fertilizer, after all, like a good friend.

So much for the history of Las Vegas.

General
Information

One of the first things you will notice when you arrive in Las Vegas by plane, car, or bus is that—aside from a few alleys in the older downtown section—this is one of the cleanest cities in the United States. There is a good reason for this: Las Vegas was created solely to be a resort city, and the city administrators know that keeping the city clean is one of the things that encourage tourists to return.

Like all major American cities, Las Vegas has a problem with crime, but the FBI figures on the city may be deceptively high. Because of the very nature of Las Vegas —gambling and a lot of money floating around—the city attracts certain types of crime, such as pickpocketing and prostitution. Tourists will find that the areas they frequent the most—the Strip and the Downtown—are brightly lighted and well patroled, as are the large hotel parking lots. Still, a few cautions are in order:

• Don't flash your money about ostentatiously— particularly if you are a heavy bettor or high roller.

- Know where your purse or wallet is at all times. Don't get so carried away by your gambling that you forget your purse on the floor. Others may have an eye on it.

- Don't leave valuables in your room. Sometimes the hotels change the locks when a key is missing; sometimes they don't.

- In the downtown area, stick to the main drag.

DOWNTOWN LAS VEGAS

There are actually two Las Vegases: the older downtown section, where it all began back in 1905; and the newer, more expensive area known as the "Strip."

The downtown area, along Fremont Street from Main Street to Las Vegas Boulevard, is only four blocks long—but what a four blocks! In fact, it may be the most famous four blocks in the entire world, even though it is now showing signs of wear. It has often been used as the backdrop for movies and television shows, such as *VEGA$*.

This section of Las Vegas—also known as "Glitter Gulch" or "Casino Center"—is undoubtedly the most brightly lighted stretch of real estate in the entire world. Dazzling neon seems to be moving in all directions. In fact, it is so bright that you can easily read a newspaper there at 4 A.M.

On New Year's Eve, this four-block area is cordoned off and turned into one great big block party.

The hotels downtown tend to be cheaper than those along the Strip. On the other hand, big-name entertainment is not offered, other than at the newly redeveloped Golden Nugget Hotel, under the direction of Las Vegas' financial whiz kid Steve Wynn. Such entertainers as Willie Nelson and even Frank Sinatra play there, Sinatra having been signed to a long-term contract by Wynn.

Professional gamblers feel that they get a better shake, that the odds are better, in the downtown area.

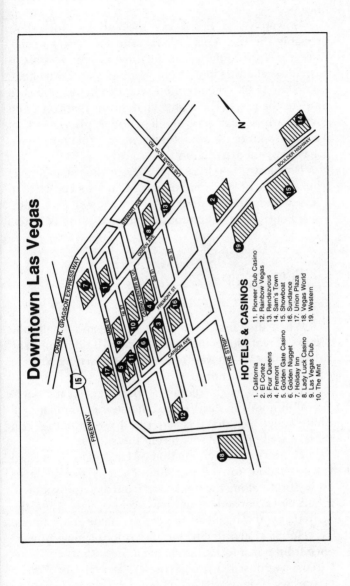

Downtown Las Vegas

HOTELS & CASINOS

1. California
2. El Cortez
3. Four Queens
4. Fremont
5. Golden Gate Casino
6. Golden Nugget
7. Holiday Inn
8. Lady Luck Casino
9. Las Vegas Club
10. The Mint
11. Pioneer Club Casino
12. Rainbow Vegas
13. Rendezvous
14. Sam's Town
15. Showboat
16. Sundance
17. Union Plaza
18. Vegas World
19. Western

Certainly the drinks are cheaper—and free, of course, to players.

Downtown is also home to Binion's Horseshoe, probably the real gambler's favorite Las Vegas casino. Binion's is the only casino in the city where there is virtually no betting limit. Your first bet is your only limit: If you bet $5,000 the first time, you can bet $5,000 each time for the rest of the night. That means that you could come in with a quarter of a million dollars in cash and bet it on one spin of the roulette wheel. As a matter of fact, it has happened at Binion's.

Downtown hotels in the order of their appearance from the foot of Fremont Street at Main Street are: Union Plaza (where Amtrak stops), Golden Nugget, Mint, Binion's, Four Queens, Fremont, Sundance, and El Cortez.

THE STRIP

When they first built on this three-and-a-half-mile section of real estate, the "smart money" said it would be a disaster because it was too far from the action. Now, of course, it *is* the action.

The Strip is the home of the biggest and most beautiful hotels in Las Vegas, but there is so much real estate in between that it is better to drive down the Strip than to walk, particularly during the summer.

The Strip is a continuation of Las Vegas Boulevard from the downtown area, although it is several miles away. It runs along the boulevard from Sahara Avenue to a half-block beyond Tropicana Avenue. It is along the Strip that you will find an array of big-name entertainers.

Hotels along the Strip in the order of their appearance from north to south are: Sahara, El Rancho, Circus Circus, Stardust, Riviera, Frontier, Desert Inn, Sands, Castaways, Caesars Palace, Imperial Palace, Flamingo Hilton, Bally's Las Vegas, Dunes, Barbary Coast, Aladdin, Marina, Tropicana, and the Hacienda.

The Las Vegas Hilton, the largest luxury resort hotel in the world (more than 3,000 rooms), is neither on the

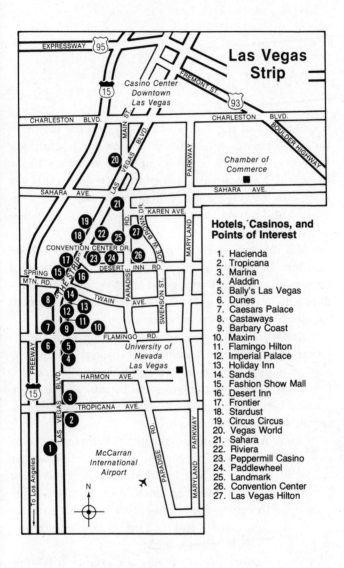

Las Vegas Strip

Hotels, Casinos, and Points of Interest

1. Hacienda
2. Tropicana
3. Marina
4. Aladdin
5. Bally's Las Vegas
6. Dunes
7. Caesars Palace
8. Castaways
9. Barbary Coast
10. Maxim
11. Flamingo Hilton
12. Imperial Palace
13. Holiday Inn
14. Sands
15. Fashion Show Mall
16. Desert Inn
17. Frontier
18. Stardust
19. Circus Circus
20. Vegas World
21. Sahara
22. Riviera
23. Peppermill Casino
24. Paddlewheel
25. Landmark
26. Convention Center
27. Las Vegas Hilton

Strip nor in the downtown area but on Paradise Road, which is a block or so from the Strip.

WHAT TO PACK

Because of the nature of the city and the nature of the environment—sunny nearly all year and hot much of the year—Las Vegas is one of the most informal cities in the world. No show room or restaurant requires that you wear a tie, although some of them would like you to wear a jacket and refrain from wearing a swimsuit to the show or in the restaurant.

But informal dress is the bane of the American on vacation. If you are going to spend all that money for dinner—and you will at a good Las Vegas restaurant—then why not dress up for it? Let the diner complement the dinner. Make a special occasion of it.

Bring your swimsuit, of course, along with suntan lotion. Bring informal summer wear throughout the year and perhaps a sweater if you come during January or February. Bring your dressiest duds, too, as the more opulent casinos now have some of the most upscale restaurants in the Western U.S.

There is something about a luxury resort that makes you feel romantic. The casinos have no windows or clocks, so that you won't know what time of day it is. People stay up around the clock here, and that does something to you. So bring something romantic to wear.

Bring your camera and read up on how to take pictures of the lavish lights at night.

And, of course, bring money and credit cards—but don't *ever* expect to get a personal check cashed in Las Vegas. Don't they trust you? They don't trust anyone. They've been scammed too often. Finally, bring your gambling budget—and stick to it.

SEASONAL EVENTS

Las Vegas is not really a town for seasonal events, since—other than the two weeks before Christmas—it is on a roll all year round, but there are a few, and they are worth mentioning.

Probably the most famous is the Mint 400 Off-Road Desert Race, which was immortalized by gonzo-journalist Hunter S. Thompson in his famous *Fear and Loathing in Las Vegas.* The race occurs annually around the end of May.

The Mint Hotel was not too fond of the book, but it remains the funniest tome ever written about Las Vegas. The *best* book about Las Vegas, in case you're interested, is Larry McMurtry's *Desert Rose.* It's a book in which a showgirl is the heroine.

The only other seasonal event worth mentioning is Helldorado (which occurs around the time that the Mint 400 is winding up), devoted to the Wild West, rodeo, and general whooping-it-up.

GETTING THERE

By Plane. At last count, Las Vegas was served by 14 airlines: American, Braniff, Continental, Delta, Eastern, Hawaiian, Northwest Orient, PSA, Republic, Southwest, Sun World, TWA, and United; and from Canada, Republic and Western. There are no direct flights from Mexico, alas, although there should be, considering all the Las Vegas traffic that comes from south of the border.

A limo from the airport to Strip hotels costs $2.75; to downtown hotels, $4.25. For private limousine service, expect to pay a minimum of $20.

By Car. You can get to Las Vegas via U.S. 93 from the east (nearest major city is Kingman, Arizona), U.S. 95 from the north (coming down from Reno or San Francisco), or I–15 from Los Angeles from the west or Salt Lake City from the north. There are no major routes from the south.

By Train. Las Vegas has the only railroad station in the world that is actually in a gambling casino! The Union Plaza Hotel was built downtown on the site of the old Union Pacific train station, so when Amtrak decided to make a stop in Las Vegas, it was only logical that the new station be located right where the old one had been. Consequently, when you jump off Amtrak, you're right in the heart of the Union Plaza Hotel casino.

You can get to Las Vegas via Amtrak from Los Angeles—about an 8-hour trip if the train is running on time—or from Salt Lake City, Denver, Chicago, or even as far away as New York City.

By Bus. Las Vegas is served by Greyhound, with stations next to the Union Plaza and on the Strip, next door to the Stardust Hotel. Ask the bus driver about it if you are going to be staying at a hotel on the Strip. A lot of people don't know about that one, and it can save you the cost of a taxi to your hotel.

WEATHER

Good Day, Sunshine. Since Las Vegas is located in the desert Southwest, its climate is mild. On the average, the city receives less than 4 inches of rain a year, and visitors can expect sunshine 86 percent of the time.

During the summer months, the daytime temperature may climb above 100 degrees, although with very low humidity. The temperature often drops no more than 10 to 15 degrees after the sun goes down.

Spring and fall produce pleasant temperatures in the 70s and 80s. Winters also are mild, with daytime temperatures in the 50s and 60s. But evening temperatures may dip to near or even slightly below freezing.

Winter's Wonders. Since it is exciting to live in the sunbelt, Las Vegas has become one of the fastest-growing cities in the nation. Consequently, if you drive around town, you will see building going on everywhere: houses, apartments, stores, and shopping centers.

Many of the newer houses and apartments, you will notice, have fireplaces, as more people move here from the East and West. Fireplaces in Las Vegas? In the middle of the desert? Are these people crazy? The rational answer to your question is: Yes, they are all crazy. That's why they move to Las Vegas. They like intense heat, and they like fireplaces. There is no other reasonable explanation for it, so don't look for one.

Perhaps another aspect of the same phenomenon is the snow: there is none. Or rather, there is snow no more often than once in 5 years in Las Vegas, and even then, it only lasts for a few minutes.

Yet Las Vegans like snow. Every so often during the winter, especially around Christmastime, they go to visit the snow, either in nearby Mount Charleston (30 miles away), where there is a ski resort, or up in Utah, where there is the excellent ski resort Brianhead. They *visit* the snow. Then they come back.

TIME/PHONES

Las Vegas is in the Pacific time zone, the same as Los Angeles. That's 3 hours earlier than eastern time. The time zone changes at Hoover Dam, Arizona, to mountain time—one hour later.

The telephone area code for the entire state of Nevada is 702. Pay-station telephone calls in Las Vegas now cost a quarter. In the event that you run into an emergency during your stay in Las Vegas, here are a few useful telephone numbers:

Addiction Treatment, 383–1347
Alcoholics Anonymous, 382–9424
Child Abuse, 366–1640
Consumer Affairs, 386–5293
Emergency Medical and Fire, 911
Gamblers Anonymous, 385–7732

Mental Health, 870–7211
Poison Information, 385–1277
Police, 795–3111
Rape Crisis Center, 735–1111
Road Conditions, 385–0181
Secret Witness Hotline, 386–3213
Suicide Prevention, 731–2990

GETTING AROUND

Las Vegas is definitely not a walker's city. The hotels are too far apart; downtown is too far from the Strip; and much of the year, it's just too hot to walk. Bring comfortable walking shoes only if you feel you must walk somewhere. Otherwise take a taxicab; that's how people get around here.

Well, actually, it is not entirely true that no one in Las Vegas walks. When the weather is cool during the winter months, a lengthy stroll along the Strip can be rather pleasant in the evening. But during the summer, only a masochist would attempt it.

If you are not familiar with desert weather, you may recall that in your grade-school geography book you read that the desert is "blistering hot during the day and freezing cold during the night." Balderdash! That may be true of the high desert, but in places such as Las Vegas, it is hot during the day and hot during the night. The nighttime temperature drops about 10–15 degrees. So if it was 115 degrees during the day—which is not an unusual summer temperature in Las Vegas—does that mean you want to walk around in 100-degree heat at night? Nonsense.

Taxicabs are plentiful and relatively inexpensive. Use them. Since Las Vegas is still a small city, nothing is very far from anything else. The Strip hotels are only a $7 taxi ride from the airport; downtown hotels are about $11; and the ride from downtown hotels to Strip hotels costs about $7.

The city of Las Vegas also provides a convenient **bus**

service that runs along the Strip and into the downtown area. The buses come along every few minutes, and the fare is $1. (Make sure you have the right change; the driver does not make change). The drive at night is quite spectacular.

Renting a Car. The easiest places to rent a car in Las Vegas are at the airport, at your hotel, or at various locations on the Strip. The major ones are:

Airways—airport, 798–6100
Allstate—airport, 736–6147
Avis—airport, 739–5595; Caesars Palace, 731–7790; Hilton, 734–8081; Bally's Las Vegas, 736–1935; (800) 331–1212
Budget—airport, 736–1212; (800) 527–0700
Dollar—airport, 739–8408
Hertz—airport, 736–4900; Desert Inn, 735–4597; Union Plaza, 383–0843; (800) 654–3131
National—airport, 739–5391; Aladdin, 739–5391; Golden Nugget, 384–5787; Imperial Palace, 732–9108; Marina, 736–0980; Sahara, 369–5783; Stardust, 733–8997
Thrifty—airport, 736–4706; 328–4567

You will find car-rental prices to be comparable with other cities.

Two driving tips: Since Las Vegas is a city where there are no closing hours for the sale or consumption of liquor, it is also a city where the driving can be a little hazardous, day or night, so drive defensively. Also, all cars in Las Vegas are air-conditioned—they have to be because of the desert heat—and sometimes the start-and-stop driving around the city can overheat your radiator, so use the fan on your air conditioners at a moderate level.

GUIDED TOURS

Las Vegas is more than just the Gambling Mecca of the World. It is also the hub of a variety of interesting sights and trips, and the tourist with limited time can save a lot of that time by taking one or more of the many tours available. Tours allow the visitor to enjoy Las Vegas' dazzling entertainment and nightlife without having to worry about traffic, parking, or reservations.

The guided tours concentrate on two areas: the famed Strip and its fabulous shows; and the lesser-known periphery of the city, which includes Hoover Dam, Lake Mead, Death Valley, and even the Grand Canyon, which is a scant 300 miles away, a short driving distance in the Southwest.

For those who like to have their evening planned for them, there are **city and nightclub tours** loaded with shows and rides through the flashing fantasyland of the fabulous Strip and downtown's Glitter Gulch. One major benefit of these prearranged "parties" is that there is no long wait in the show-room line. A tour guide will insure your prompt seating.

You probably will want to take your camera along on the tour for some of those classic Vegas nighttime-neon shots, but be forewarned that cameras are not permitted in any of the show rooms. If you have your camera with you, be prepared to check it at the door.

One of the most popular excursions in Las Vegas is the half-day tour of **Hoover Dam,** the highest concrete dam in the western hemisphere. An air-conditioned bus will whisk you to this 727-foot-high engineering marvel. Once there, you can take an elevator down into the bowels of this Colorado River fortress and see just how the hydroelectric powerhouse works. A Hoover Dam tour also can include a one-hour boat cruise to the upstream side of the dam for lunch.

Companies offering tours in and around Las Vegas are *Gray Line Tours* (384–1234) and *All State Tour & Travel*

(798–5002, 798–5606 or 800–634–6787). Call for prices and other information.

A number of airlines fly over and through the **Grand Canyon.** Among them are *Adventure Airlines* (736–7511); *Lake Mead Air* (293–1848); *Las Vegas Airlines* (647–3056); and *Scenic Airlines* (739–1900).

Scenic Airlines is the pioneer in this business and undoubtedly offers the most popular air tours. Within minutes after take off, you'll pass over the massive Hoover Dam and the upper reaches of Lake Mead. Then, before you know it, you'll swoop down below the rim of the Grand Canyon for an aerial view of the tall eroded plateaus that are seldom seen in any other way because of the area's inaccessibility.

Camera buffs will find this flight to be a special delight since the planes have only window seats, which afford everyone a close-up view of this unparalleled panorama. The plane soars over extinct volcanoes, lava flows, canyon waterfalls, and even an active Indian village. Native Americans began inhabiting this area 300 years before Columbus discovered North America, and several Indian tribes, including the Havasupai, still call this area home.

Some of the flights land at the Grand Canyon Airport, where ground transportation will take you to a nearby inn for lunch. Then, it's a visit to the breathtaking precipice known as the "south rim." At an elevation of 7,000 feet, it is usually much cooler than Las Vegas, so take along a sweater.

The Scenic Airlines roundtrip tour is $126 per person or, with ground transportation, $176 per person. The tour is offered in several languages.

Two-day (overnight) tours to the Grand Canyon also are offered by *LTR Stage Lines* (384–1230); *Gray Line Motor Tours* (384–1234); and *Greyhound Tours* (382–2640). Fares are about $85 per person.

Most of the tours will provide free pickup and return to your hotel.

For water enthusiasts, there is a pleasurable cruise of **Lake Mead,** the largest man-made lake in the western hemisphere. Located at the Lake Mead Marina, just 45 minutes from Las Vegas, the craft will glide over the lake to within a few hundred yards of Hoover Dam's upstream face. The tour guide also will point out historic shoreline landmarks. The boat tour leaves the marina four times daily. Call *Lake Mead Yacht Tours* (736–6180).

You also can rent fishing boats, ski boats, and even houseboats at most of the Lake Mead marinas. For information on boat rental call *Lake Mead Resort* (293–2074); *Echo Bay Resort* (394–4000); or *Temple Bar Resort* (602–767 –3400).

(Hoover Dam marks the boundary between Nevada and Arizona, and some of the lake's resorts are on the Arizona side.)

Try a one-day **raft trip** on the Colorado River, just below Hoover Dam. No white water, just mild drifting, but a delight for camera buffs. Eleven miles (3 hours) through Black Canyon, with waterfalls, hot springs, and, of course, the dam. $49.50, adults; $25, children under 12. Call *Black Canyon Inc.* (293–3679).

ARCHITECTURE

You may find this a little hard to believe, but Las Vegas has been cited by a prominent group of architects for the "unity and inventiveness of its design." The things they have called attention to most include the imaginative use of neon, lights, glass, and space. They have noted that unlike most cities, Las Vegas is all of one piece architecturally, because it is a relatively new city, created for one purpose only. And according to these architects, it works. Particular examples cited were:

- Caesars Palace's entranceway and its Omnimax dome —in fact, the entire building;
- Flamingo Hilton's neon sign;
- the conservation of energy in the facade of the Stardust hotel;
- the use of color on the Circus Circus marquee;
- the entire bigger-than-life effect of Glitter Gulch (downtown area);

- casinos of the Tropicana Hotel, Bally's Las Vegas, and the Golden Nugget.

So, if you always secretly loved the way that Las Vegas looked but were too embarrassed to admit it, you can relax. The way it looks has been certified by architects.

PHOTO OPPORTUNITIES

Las Vegas is a photographer's dream. Nowhere else in the world is there so much color and action in one place. With just a little care, you can go home with pictures that make your friends exclaim: "How did you get that?!"

The summer sun is so bright that if you are operating anything other than an Instamatic, a film speed no higher than 100 ASA is recommended. If you are going to take some night shots of the signs—and you certainly should—a fast film speed (400 or 1,000 ASA) is recommended. Just ask a local photo shop what type of exposure they would recommend. An f-stop of four at 1/60 of a second with 400 ASA color film is not a bad choice.

Ten great photo opportunities:
1) The Flamingo Hilton sign
2) The entrance to Caesars Palace
3) The fountain in front of the Bally's Las Vegas
4) A view of the Strip from the 26th floor restaurant-lounge of the Dunes Hotel
5) The front of the Holiday Casino, day or night
6) The front of Circus Circus casino, day or night
7) The Stardust Hotel marquee
8) The front of the El Rancho hotel, day or night
9) View of the Strip from the glass-enclosed elevator at the Desert Inn

10) View overlooking the downtown area from Union Plaza Centre Stage restaurant.

MUSEUMS

Believe it or not, there are such things as museums in Las Vegas. Here are a few you may consider as a quiet respite from the glitter:

University of Nevada, Las Vegas Natural History Museum exhibits a collection of flora and fauna that have made southern Nevada their home. 4505 Maryland Pkwy. near the Strip (739–3381). Mon.–Fri., 8:30 A.M.–5 P.M. Free.

Murals of area history and early mementos of the west are featured at **Nevada State Museum and Historical Society,** 700 Twin Lakes Dr. (385–0115). Open every day of the year, 9 A.M.–4 P.M.; Admission $1 adults, 50¢ children and seniors.

Las Vegas Art Museum highlights painters and artists of the West. 3333 W. Washington St. (647–4300). Free.

Lost City Museum. Artifacts of prehistoric Indians who inhabited the area and a full-scale model of an Indian pueblo can be seen 60 miles northeast of Las Vegas. Take I–15 north to the Overton cutoff to the right (397–2193). Open year round, 8 A.M.–5 P.M. Free.

Liberace Museum is devoted to the piano memorabilia of the late showman: pianos, cars, works of art, and costumes that have to be seen to be believed. In the Liberace Plaza, 1775 E. Tropicana Ave. (798–5595). Daily, 10 A.M.–5 P.M. and Sunday, 1–5 P.M. Donation to the Liberace Foundation of the Creative and Performing Arts: $3.50 adults, $2 children under 12.

No gambling here

The newest addition to the Las Vegas scene is **Wet 'n' Wild,** 2535 Las Vegas Blvd. S., right next to the Sahara Hotel on the Strip (737–3819). Just the place to drop the kids for a summer day, Wet 'n' Wild is a 26-acre water park that has everything from the terrifying Der Stuka, a 76-foot free fall down a watery chute, to a float trip along a one-third-mile river. Flumes, slides, water cannons, and rapids. 10 A.M.–9 P.M. during the summer. $11.

Yes, Las Vegas actually does have a zoo—the **Southern Nevada Zoological Park.** It's not very large, but it is there. The zoo houses apes, tigers, leopards, lions, and other animals, plus a petting zoo. 1775 N. Rancho Dr. (648–5955). Mon.-Sat. 9 A.M.–6 P.M.; Sun 9 A.M.–5 P.M. Admission $2.50 adults, $1.50 children under 16 and seniors.

Ripley's Believe It or Not, right next to the Four Queens Hotel (385–4011), has all of the fantastic things you would expect to see in a Ripley exhibit—4,000 of them.

Omnimax Theater, Caesars Palace, 3570 Las Vegas Blvd. (731–7900). The movie theater of the future, with a nearly wraparound screen and scores of speakers and special movies taken just for this technique. Hourly, 11 A.M.–midnight. $3, adults; $2, children and seniors.

One of the best car museums in the world is the **Imperial Palace Car Collection** at the Imperial Palace, 3535 Las Vegas Blvd. S. (731–3311). More than 200 classic, antique, and special-interest cars. Includes Hitler's 1939 Mercedes, the King of Siam's 1928 Delage, a 1930 Cord, a 1931 V–12 Cadillac, and many more. Open daily, 9:30 A.M.–11:30 P.M. $3.75, adults; $2, children and seniors.

Circus Circus Hotel Mezzanine, 2880 Las Vegas Blvd. S. (734–0410). Live circus acts perform day and night over the heads of the gamblers in the casino, while the mezzanine is like a circus midway, with more games for kids than you have ever seen in your life.

THIS SPORTING LIFE

When one thinks of Las Vegas and sporting events, a number of events come to mind: World Class Boxing at Caesars Palace and the Las Vegas Hilton; great Tennis Classics at Caesars; the famed Mint 400 Off Road Desert Race.

But none of these will come to the mind of a Las Vegan as quickly as the basketball games of the University of Nevada at Las Vegas Running Rebels. Coach Jerry Tarkanian throws 'em all into his famous Shark Tank and they usually come out winners. The Running Rebels' games are held in the new Thomas and Mack Center on the campus, which is not far from the Strip. Call 739-3267 about tickets.

Other Las Vegas sporting events include the Helldorado Rodeo (June) and the National Finals Rodeo (December).

Among the internationally known sports figures who have battled it out in Las Vegas are John McEnroe, Muhammad Ali, George Foreman, Larry Holmes, Jack Nicklaus, Sugar Ray Leonard, Nancy Lopez—the list is endless.

Many people do not realize that Las Vegas has its own baseball team, the Las Vegas Stars, a professional triple-A farm club for the San Diego Padres. They play at Cashman Field, 850 Las Vegas Blvd. N. (386–7200).

Additional major sporting events that are repeated every year are:

- $250,000 Alan King Tennis Classic—April
- Las Vegas Panasonic Pro-Celebrity Golf Classic—July
- U.S. Open Bass Tournament (again, the world's richest)—September
- Caesars Palace Grand Prix—October.

In addition to these regular events, Las Vegas is chosen time and again as the site for major boxing, golf, tennis, or body-building events. There are 11 golf courses in the city and 18 tennis facilities.

The professionals are not the only ones who can enjoy sport in Las Vegas. There are ample facilities for everyone. Each hotel has its own swimming pool, of course, and with an average of 320 days of sunshine a year, the weather is nearly always good for sports.

GOLF COURSES

If you enjoy golf, you should not deny yourself that pleasure while you are in Las Vegas, since the climate provides you with ideal golfing weather. The summer months tend to be a *little* hot, but the rest of the year is wonderful. Some of the hotel courses are most attractive. Here are a few of the best courses:

Desert Inn Country Club, Desert Inn Hotel, 3145 Las Vegas Blvd. S. (733–4299); par 72; yardage 7,089.
Dunes Country Club, Dunes Hotel, 3650 Las Vegas Blvd. S. (737–4749); par 72; yardage 7,240.
Las Vegas Municipal Golf Course., Decatur and Washington blvds. (646–3003); par 72; yardage 6,607.
Sahara Country Club, 1911 Desert Inn Rd. (796–0016); par 71; yardage 6,761.
Tropicana Country Club, Tropicana Hotel, 3801 Las Vegas Blvd. S. (739–2457); par 70; yardage 6,647.
Showboat Country Club, 1 Green Valley Pkwy. (451–2106); par 71; yardage 6967.

TENNIS, ANYONE?

As with golf, you will find Las Vegas to be an ideal city for tennis. Here are some of the best courts:

Caesars Palace (731–7786). Six outdoor courts; world champion Pancho Gonzalez is the pro here; hotel guests and the public, if space is available.

Desert Inn (733–4577). Ten outdoor courts, all lighted; hotel guests and public.

Dunes Hotel (737–4493). Five outdoor courts, two lighted; hotel guests and public.

Frontier Hotel (734–0110). Two outdoor courts, both lighted; hotel guests and public.

Hacienda Hotel (739–8911). Six courts, two lighted; hotel guests and public. (739–4111). Ten outdoor courts, four lighted; hotel guests have priority.

Riviera Hotel (734–5538). Four courts, all lighted; hotel guests and public.

Sands Hotel (733–5000). Six lighted courts; hotel guests and public.

Stardust Hotel (732–6460). Four courts; hotel guests and public.

Tropicana Hotel (739–2439). Eight courts, all indoors; climate controlled; hotel guests and public.

Union Plaza (386–2110). Four courts, all lighted; open to all.

TIPPING

Las Vegas is a town that lives on "green grease" more than any place in the world. You can get anything here—if you know the right people and have the right money. But even if you have never been to Las Vegas before, you can ease your way around town with the judicious placing of a little green. Here's how to distribute it:

Valet parker—$1 is expected at the better hotels. The parkers all look like John Travolta and drive like Evel Knievel. They probably make more money than you do.

Bellman, porter—$1, unless special services are required. A $10 tip will provide you with a solid information source.

Waiter—the usual 15 percent unless the service has been exceptional, which in Las Vegas is not uncommon. Then, 20 percent is not out of order.

Maître d' at the show room—Las Vegas is one town where the early bird definitely does not get the worm. The type of seat you get in a show room has *nothing* to do with your place in the line. You can arrive 5 minutes before the show starts and get the best seat in the house. What has everything to do with where you sit and how you are treated is how well you grease the maître d's palm when you come in. For most shows, if you are two or four people, a $20 bill should get you a nice booth. Naturally, the price escalates as the performer escalates. Expect to tip more for Frank Sinatra or Julio Iglesias.

If you are unhappy over where you are sitting, don't complain loudly about it. Merely summon one of the captains, press $10 in his hand and tell him you would like to sit somewhere else—or point to where you would like to sit.

Dealer—It is customary when you are winning to tip the dealer a chip or two of what you are playing. A dealer at a good house in Las Vegas can make between $50,000 and $100,000 a year, and "hustling for tips" is against the rules. Why then are they never smiling? They will tell you it is because the job is hard, often boring, and they frequently have to deal with people who are in a very bad mood. That doesn't sound like sufficient reason to us.

Room attendant—America is a land where it is not customary to tip the housekeeper, and it's a shame, for they work hard for the money. Leave them a little something; $1 a day in the better hotels would not be out of line.

Keno runner—Here again, something proportional when you are winning.

Pool attendant—50¢ or $1.

Cocktail waitress in the casino—Since the drinks are free to players, $1 tip per round is usually expected.

INFORMATION SOURCES

The best sources for information about Las Vegas are the **Las Vegas Chamber of Commerce,** 2301 E. Sahara Ave., Las Vegas, Nev. 89104 (457–4664); and the **Las Vegas Convention and Visitors Authority,** Convention Center, Las Vegas, 89109 (733–2323). They can provide you with maps, lists of hotels and their prices, informational booklets, and in some cases, discount coupon books for the casinos.

A word about coupon books, which are also called "fun books." They are booklets of coupons, usually put together by the small "grind joints." The larger hotels do not use them. With one of these coupon books, you can get everything from a free breakfast to a free pull of a slot machine. But for the most part, they are not really worth the trouble, unless you are down on your luck and really need that free breakfast. The gimmick is, if you want to use more than one coupon out of the book, you have to stay in the casino for some time; they are like time-release capsules. Still, some people like them, particularly senior citizens. The best fun book you will find in Las Vegas is the one you are holding in your hand.

CITY OF LIGHTS

During the energy crunch a few years ago, a number of people pointed an accusing finger at Las Vegas and declared: "Look! Conspicuous consumption. Make them turn the lights off!" And Las Vegas did—for a while. But not for long. You want the lights to be on *somewhere* in America, don't you? Well then, what better place than Las Vegas, a city that was designed only for having fun?

Actually, the consumption of electricity here is much less than you would think, and most of the signs are quite conservative of energy. Still, there is no denying that Las Vegas is T*H*E M*O*S*T B*R*I*G*H*T*L*Y

L*I*G*H*T*E*D   C*I*T*Y   I*N   T*H*E
W*O*R*L*D. In fact, only a fifth of one percent of all
the power generated by the Nevada Power Company
goes to light the signs that have made Las Vegas what it
is, and *all* of the power used by *all* of the hotels for *all* of
their purposes only amounts to about 10 percent of what
Nevada Power generates. So there. Also, the power is
relatively cheap because of the proximity of Hoover
Dam.

So stop tsk-tsking and just enjoy it.

LIGHTS! CAMERA! ACTION!

Las Vegas probably gets more attention from Hollywood than any city outside of Los Angeles. For one thing,
it is only 300 miles from Los Angeles. For another, the
movies and TV like a place with a lot of color, and Las
Vegas certainly has that.

In any given week, there usually will be at least one
movie and several TV programs being shot in the city.
Watching a movie being made can be both exciting and
boring at the same time. Look! Over there! Isn't that
Ryan O'Neal with Farrah? Yes, as a matter of fact, it is.
What is he doing? Nothing. He's studying his script and
waiting for something to happen. That's probably what
he will be doing for the next 2 hours. If you watch a
movie in production, you wonder how it *ever* gets made.
All it seems to be is: sit around and wait. Or, if something
is happening, it will be Sylvester Stallone—all five feet
seven inches of him—crying to Apollo Creed, "Get up
and win that fight!" Unfortunately, the room where the
movie is being made is so large that Stallone's deep voice
comes across as being small and unimpressive. Without
background music, editing, and everything else that goes
into moviemaking, you think the film is going to be terri-
ble. Then, when you finally see it in a theater, you think:
This movie is *great!*

The magic of Hollywood.

The two hotels that seem to attract the most attention from the movies and from TV specials are Caesars Palace and Bally's Las Vegas. So, if you would like to see a movie or a TV show being made—and don't say we didn't warn you—call the Chamber of Commerce (457-4664), the Las Vegas News Bureau (735-3611), or the Nevada Film Commission (386-5287).

SEEING STARS

If you think that was Sean Penn walking across the casino of Caesars Palace with Madonna on his arm, or that that was Shirley MacLaine sitting in the deli eating a ham-on-rye, you are probably right. At any given time, there are a lot of superstars playing up and down the Strip, and since Los Angeles is so near, Las Vegas is very popular as a quick escape for the stars.

You can get an autograph, if you so desire, but one of the reasons the stars like Las Vegas is that they feel they can let their hair down here and just be one of the crowd. For the most part, visitors gawk, but they usually don't bother the celebrities. Before you ask someone for an autograph, ask yourself if you *really* need it, or is it just something to prove that you met the star, a scrap of paper that will later be dropped in a drawer and forgotten. By not pestering them for an autograph, you put yourself on the same sophisticated level that they are on.

PACKAGE DEALS

One of the ways to save a little money and get some bonuses when you come to Las Vegas is through package deals. All the hotels have them, so you should ask your hotel to send you information about their "standard package" and any "special packages" they may have at the time. Because some of the package deals during soft (slow) times of the year are incredible bargains, they are not advertised heavily, although they are publicized through travel agents. The hotel wants to sell the packages, but it also wants to preserve its luxury impression by not advertising itself as a bargain hotel. In other words, even places such as Caesars Palace, Bally's Las Vegas, and the Las Vegas Hilton have packages.

A typical package will include a deluxe room for two nights for two persons, admission to the hotel show, a couple of drinks in the hotel lounge, a keno ticket, and maybe a pull on a special slot machine. During soft periods of the year, a special package may provide you with a luxury hotel room for half what you were expecting to pay.

JUNKETS

In connection with Las Vegas, you may hear the term "junket," and you may wonder what it is.

First of all, a junket is not a custard. It is a trip to Las Vegas that has been arranged by the casino junket director. These trips are not as plentiful today as they were in the past, and not as many hotels provide them. The reasons are twofold: the increasing cost of airfare; and the increasing convention business that is filling up those junket spaces. Still, junkets are sometimes arranged for high rollers—or for people who want to be.

Contrary to what you may think, the hotel does not really care whether the junketeer goes home a winner or a loser. If he loses, all well and good; that's what the hotel is there for. If he goes home a winner, also well and good. He will become a walking advertisement for the hotel. The important thing is that he is willing to push the expected money across the table.

The junket usually includes such things as free roundtrip airfare, free room, free meals, and free shows. In return for that—for, say, a three-day trip—the player may be expected to push $7,000–$10,000 across the table with minimum bets of $25–$50. Of course, there is no reason why he cannot go home with more money than he brought. Again, all well and good. He'll come back next time—and perhaps not be as lucky.

If you are going to be invited back again, you should be able to lose gracefully and not break up the place just because they took your money or question the legitimacy of birth of the casino manager. Casinos recognize there is no such thing as a good loser. ("Show me a good loser, and I'll show you a loser," someone once said.) But at least, you should be able to lose more or less gracefully.

The junket was invented in the mid-sixties by Morris Lansburgh, the colorful operator of the Flamingo Hotel. Lansburgh saw all that East Coast gambling money going to the Caribbean, solely because of the higher airfare to Las Vegas. If the hotels took care of the airfare and other essentials, he reasoned, then the gamblers would come.

Lansburgh talked to Kirk Kerkorian, who was then a struggling airline operator, about private charter flights for high rollers. He offered to charter Kerkorian's vintage Trans International Airlines to bring gamblers to Las Vegas. Kerkorian became the principal stockholder in Bally's Las Vegas (formerly the MGM Grand Hotel), so the idea must have worked.

VACATION CERTIFICATES

No, no, no. If someone calls you long distance from Las Vegas and offers you a "vacation certificate" worth $500 in rooms, meals, and other goodies in Las Vegas—

if you send them only $50—hang up. These outfits are known as "boiler-room operations," using WATS lines to make cheap calls all over the country. They will provide you with what usually can be obtained free when you get here (in the form of coupon books) or with "room certificates" that are not honored by the hotels because they have never heard of the outfit that sold them to you. The city is trying to close down these boiler-room operations. In the meantime, beware.

MONEY CHANGERS

Being a worldwide tourist destination, Las Vegas gets a lot of foreign visitors. Visitors need have no fear that they won't be able to change their money in Las Vegas. (Within reason, of course. Don't produce bills from a country that has just had a coup.) Some major hotel casinos are able to exchange foreign currency from major countries. In addition to the airport, here is where you can find the money changers:

American Foreign Exchange of Nevada, Las Vegas Hilton Hotel (731–4155).
Nevada Coin Mart, 750 E. Sahara Ave., near the Sahara Hotel (369–0500).
Valley Bank of Nevada, 101 Convention Center Dr., near the convention center (386–1417).

PARKING

One of the real plusses of Las Vegas is that ample free parking is available at the hotels all over the city. There is plenty of room in Las Vegas, and the hotel parking lots are very large. On the other hand, you may want to avail yourself of valet parking, which is available at each hotel. There is no charge for this service, but you are expected to tip the valet parker about $1.

THE SAD STORY
OF "VEGAS VIC"

For years, Vegas Vic—a big neon cowboy sign—was a Las Vegas institution. He stood at the very center of the colorful downtown area. Visitors knew Vegas Vic from his famous "Howdy Partner," which he would repeat every minute or so, day and night.

Comes now a famous movie director, Richard Brooks, who is staying in Las Vegas with his company while making the film *The Professionals,* with Burt Lancaster and Racquel Welch. Also appearing in the movie was Lee Marvin, who decided that he didn't like Vegas Vic, he especially did not like Vegas Vic's "Howdy Partner," and most of all, he did not like Vegas Vic's "Howdy Partner" all through the night. So, throwing open his hotel window, Marvin whipped out a bow and some arrows used in the film and proceeded to shoot Vegas Vic full of holes.

Shortly after that, the city decided to shut Vegas Vic up.

GETTING MARRIED

At one time, Reno—the only other major city in Nevada—was known as "The Divorce Capital of America." Now, both Reno *and* Las Vegas could be known as "The Marriage Capitals of America," since there are ten times more weddings performed in each city than divorces. There are, in fact, about 55,000 weddings performed annually in Las Vegas.

Getting married in Las Vegas is simplicity itself, and

a lot of famous people have done it: Elizabeth Taylor and Richard Burton, Eddie Fisher and Debbie Reynolds, Frank Sinatra, Mickey Rooney, Judy Garland, Rita Hayworth, Betty Grable, Ann Miller, Rhonda Fleming and, most recently, Joan Collins.

Nevada marriage laws are quite liberal. There is no blood test or waiting period. All you have to do is pay $25 for a marriage license at the Clark County Clerk's office in the downtown area. While a civil ceremony costs only $25, you will find that getting married in one of Las Vegas' many chapels doesn't cost much more, since marriage is a big industry here and there is a lot of competition among the chapels.

Many of the chapels are able to offer you a video recording of the ceremony, and of course, all of them can provide flowers, music, and still photography of the event. Check the Yellow Pages for the services they offer.

The wedding chapels generally are open 7 days a week, 24 hours a day. The county clerk's office is open from 8 A.M. to midnight, Monday through Thursday, and 8 A.M. Friday until midnight on Sunday. It also is open 24 hours a day on holidays, but on Valentine's Day, you may have to wait in a long line to get your license. Valentine's Day isn't the busiest day, however. New Year's Eve is. Many couples get married then to take advantage of the tax break. Leave it to Las Vegas to think of that.

Wedding chapel fees range from $25 on up, depending on the number of extras that you want, such as flowers and photography. The clergy performing the ceremony are paid by "donations."

Another reason that getting married in Las Vegas is so popular is that no other city in the world can offer a honeymoon couple so much in the way of luxury rooms, fine dining, and exciting entertainment at such a reasonable price. Most Las Vegas hotels and motels have honeymoon suites or something similar. Just inquire.

There are 18 wedding chapels within the Las Vegas

city limits, ranging from storefronts to very nice little chapels.

Our favorite is the **Little Church of the West,** 3960 Las Vegas Blvd. S., next to the Hacienda Hotel (739–7971). It's a rustic Old West church that you might have seen in the movie *Shane.* Here is a selection of other chapels:

Candlelight Wedding Chapel, 2855 Las Vegas Blvd. S. (735–4179).

Little Chapel of the Flowers, 1717 Las Vegas Blvd. S. (735–4331).

Silver Bell Wedding Chapel, 607 Las Vegas Blvd. S. (382–3726).

Wee Kirk o' the Heather, 231 Las Vegas Blvd. S. (382–9830).

Two increasingly popular places to get married are the **Mount Charleston Inn** (872–5500) and the **Mount Charleston Lodge** (386–6899), both about 35 miles from Las Vegas.

WORKING IN LAS VEGAS

Who has not entertained the thought of chucking it all, of leaving the rat race, of getting away from all the ice and snow and moving to Las Vegas to become a dealer? Many of us have at least thoughts about it, and some of us have even acted upon it—at least the moving-to-Vegas part. This writer formerly lived in a cabin in the logging country of northern Idaho and decided one day to chuck it all and move to Las Vegas. That was 9 years ago.

A word of warning at the outset: If being a dealer is what you want, we must tell you up front that it is a very boring, tiresome job, and you are dealing with people who are often in a bad mood. It does pay well, however, particularly at the more prestigious hotels.

There are plenty of schools in Las Vegas that can teach you how to become a dealer. At most of them, veterans can even attend on the G.I. Bill if they are so entitled. After you have finished several weeks of training, the schools will try to place you. The usual procedure is to start working at one of the smaller hotels and then work your way up. Of course, it helps to know people in the bigger hotels. In Las Vegas, juice (how much power you have through influential contacts) is everything.

But there are more jobs in Las Vegas than just being a dealer. Las Vegas is a relatively easy place in which to find work, since it is a 24-hour-a-day city. That in itself puts a lot of people to work.

The weather is hot during the summer but absolutely delightful the rest of the year. There is almost no rain; you will never have to worry about snow tires again; and yes—we have to admit it—Las Vegas is an exciting place in which to live.

People who live in Las Vegas must see a lot of shows, right? Wrong! Las Vegans almost never go to hotel shows or casinos unless they have company visiting. It's like people in New York City never going to see the Empire State Building. People who live in Las Vegas go to events like basketball games at the University of Nevada or the movies. It's a big movie town.

Still, people in Las Vegas like to know that they know people who can get them "comps" into the shows any time they want. The town is very celebrity conscious and power conscious.

WINNERS' CIRCLE

Many visitors to Las Vegas seek freedom—freedom from working. And it does happen.

As a matter of fact, it happens all the time. Take one example: A young nurse from Santa Cruz, Calif., came to Las Vegas for the first time with her boyfriend. She didn't know anything about gambling but figured that the slot machines looked easy, so she played them. She had dropped only $30 into one of the progressive quarter machines when it happened: The lights started twirling, and the bells started ringing. She wasn't sure what was happening, but she assumed that the five 7's lined up in front of her must mean something. She looked up at the lighted board above the slots carousel.

"I can't believe it," she cried, "but I think I just won $26,000!"

An older woman tapped her on the shoulder. "Oh no, you didn't," she said.

"What do you mean?" the young lady asked.

"You read the sign wrong. You just won $126,000."

When she had recovered, she was asked what she would do with all that money. The young nurse replied, "Quit my job."

It's comforting to know that she had not lost her sense of priorities.

LAS VEGAS: ATLANTIC CITY WEST

At one time, little ol' Las Vegas had it all. If you wanted to gamble legally anywhere in the United States, that was where you had to go. Or to Reno.

Then, a little more than 7 years ago, along came Atlantic City, known for its annual Miss America pageant, its Monopoly-board street names, and little else. It was long past its prime, but then big casinos were built along the famed old Boardwalk. With a potential clientele of 50 million within a radius of 2 hours from Atlantic City, its success was assured before the first casino was even completed.

Casino gambling was supposed to revitalize the city, and it has done that—at least for the Boardwalk area. And it was supposed to take business away from Las Vegas, and it did—at least from among the business that used to come in from the East Coast.

But Atlantic City is Atlantic City and Las Vegas is Las

Vegas, and East and West shall not meet. There is only one Las Vegas.

If anyone tells you that Las Vegas is dying as a result of Atlantic City gambling, don't cover their bet. Come and take a look for yourself.

LAS VEGAS "NUMBERS"

The sun shines 86 percent of the time, the annual mean temperature is 66 degrees, and an average of 3.76 inches of rain falls each year.

There are more than 700 places to eat in the city.

Sixty-seven percent of the people who live in Las Vegas say that they gamble "sometimes." Some of them say they gamble only when they entertain out-of-town visitors.

The median age of residents is 32.6 years. Among adults, 53 percent are women. Sixty-six percent of the citizens are married. But there are no children in 61 percent of the households.

Most of the newcomers—27 percent—come from California, but a surprising 20 percent are from the Northeast.

The median household income is $27,448, while 34 percent of the households have incomes of $35,000 or higher.

Sixty-seven percent of the adults are employed, and 58 percent of the women work.

One fourth of the people have lived in Las Vegas for more than 20 years, thus discrediting the belief that it is a city of transients.

A FEW UNIQUE FACTS

One of the reasons people move to Las Vegas is that they can throw away their snow tires and chains: It snows only about once in five years in Las Vegas and even then it is usually gone in a few minutes.

As incredible as it may sound, there is a ski resort, Lee Canyon, only 35 miles northwest of Las Vegas, and it is active during the months of December, January, and February. Lake Mead, which was created with the formation of Hoover Dam, is only 30 miles in the other direction. So theoretically—this is only theoretical, mind you—in January, you could go snow skiing up at Lee Canyon in the morning, return to Las Vegas for lunch and a little gambling, and then go waterskiing on Lake Mead during the afternoon. There are not too many places in the United States that could boast such an adventure.

There are more churches per capita in Las Vegas than there are in just about any other American city: over 300, or about one for every 1,700 people in metropolitan Las Vegas. We don't know why, but maybe it's a guilty conscience—all that mobster money (from the past, of course) trying to come clean. Whatever the reason, there are only two times in Las Vegas: now . . . and the hereafter.

Take your choice.

LAS VEGAS TRIVIA

Did you know that . . .
- there are more than 20,000 college students attending classes in Las Vegas (at the University of Nevada)?
- the casino industry employs, directly or indirectly, 80 percent of the work force of the city?
- there are more than 48,000 slot machines in Las Vegas?

- the area is served by more than 400 taxicabs?
- more than 300 commercial flights land at or depart from McCarran International Airport each day?
- nearby Hoover Dam is more than 70 stories high?
- more than 100 million meals are served in Las Vegas each year?
- McCarran International Airport is undergoing a renovation that when complete (by the year 2000), will make the airport one of the most beautiful and advanced in the entire world?
- Las Vegas is truly a 24-hour-a-day town? You will find supermarkets, convenience stores, gas stations, and, of course, the hotels and casinos open around the clock—and just as many people in them at 5 A.M. as at 5 P.M. It is not uncommon to walk into a supermarket at 4 A.M. and find a showgirl just getting off work and still partially in costume (what there is of it), wheeling a cart and buying her groceries.

Advice from the doc: Since Las Vegas never closes, many people foolishly stay up around the clock and party. Don't do it. Las Vegas also has more than its share of heart attacks among visitors.

Also, beware of the sun during the summer. If you are not used to it, the desert sun can be a killer.

What a town!

HOW FAR TO . . . ?

If you are planning to extend your Las Vegas trip to other parts of the West, here are the driving distances to places you might consider: Baker, Calif., 93 miles; Barstow, Calif., 153 miles; Disneyland, Anaheim, Calif., 290 miles; Flagstaff, Ariz., 275 miles; Grand Canyon, North Rim, Ariz., 300 miles; Grand Canyon, South Rim, Ariz., 295 miles; Hoover Dam, Nev., 25 miles; Kingman, Ariz., 103 miles; Lake Havasu City, Ariz., 145 miles; Lake Tahoe, Calif., 470 miles; Los Angeles, Calif., 290 miles; Needles, Calif., 110 miles, Palm Springs, Calif., 280 miles; Phoenix, Ariz., 300 miles; Reno, Nev., 450 miles;

Salt Lake City, Utah, 456 miles; San Diego, Calif., 331 miles; San Francisco, Calif., 589 miles.

A LAS VEGAS LEXICON

You don't want to sound like a complete rube when you come to Las Vegas, do you? Don't you want to be able to speak Las Veganese? Well, take a quick look at this section from our own *Las Vegas Language System*, and you will speak like a native Las Vegan in a matter of minutes.

Card counter: a person who has a very good memory or a "system" that can actually bring the odds in blackjack closer to his or her favor. Card counters remember the cards that have been played in the game. They stay in the game with minimal bets of $2 or $5, whatever is required. Occasionally, when card counters feel that the remaining unplayed cards in the deck are unusually rich in tens and face cards—something that would produce an automatic blackjack—they start betting heavily, in the hopes that they will be dealt a good hand.

Many casinos discourage card counters by using a number of decks in the "shoe" that holds the cards. Others by shuffling the deck frequently. Some, however, such as Vegas World, actually welcome them, in the belief that they will attract high rollers.

Comp: short for *complimentary*. You're home free, in other words.

Eye in the sky: the false ceilings in casinos and the two-way mirrors, behind which is someone watching the gaming, primarily to keep the employees honest.

High roller: someone who is willing to gamble a lot of money. He or she can have anything wanted in Las Vegas.

Juice: Las Vegas runs on juice, or power. The more juice you have, the more power you have.

Mechanic: a cheat, primarily a slot-machine cheat. Called that because mechanics often work with mechanical devices, such as battery-operated drills.

RFB: the best thing that can happen to you in Las Vegas. It means that your room, food, and beverages are all comped.

Skimming: taking money off the top before it is recorded by casinos in their books. It's a very illegal act, only practiced by the most desperate casinos. They can lose their license over it—and thus kill the golden goose.

Stiff: someone who does not toke; to fail to toke. It is the worst possible thing you can do in Las Vegas, even worse than running over an old lady.

Toke: a tip; to tip. In Las Vegas, you are expected to toke anything that moves.

Hotels and Motels

There are more hotel and motel rooms in Las Vegas (about 60,000) than there are in just about any other city of comparable size in the United States. They range all the way from the $1,500-a-day high-roller or presidential suites down to the $15-a-day Motel 6 places.

But just because there are a lot of rooms does not mean that you can always find one. Las Vegas also is a very popular convention destination, and when a really big convention is in town, you may have some trouble finding a room and have to settle for that little motel (at the same price!) instead of the big hotel you were hoping for. The moral of the story: Reserve early. The last 2 weeks before Christmas is the only "slow" period in Las Vegas anymore.

Las Vegas is really two cities: the colorful older downtown area and the more expensive and spectacular Strip area. So before you try to reserve a room, decide which area of town you would like to stay in. Both are accessible by cab and by bus, of course.

HOW SUITE IT IS!

Las Vegas has some of the most luxurious hotel suites in the entire world. There is a good reason for this: The rooms are used by kings, presidents, movie and TV stars, and high rollers whom the hotels want to treat royally in return for taking all their money. These top-level suites range in price from around $800 a day to as much as $2,500 a day.

Despite that stiff tariff, the hotel most often does not collect for the suites, particularly in the case of high rollers. The suites are given away as part of a package to entice them there. The very best of these luxury suites are to be found at Caesars Palace, the Golden Nugget, the Desert Inn, and Bally's Las Vegas. Can you see them? Sadly, no. The hotels do not want "common folks" traipsing through their thousand-dollar rooms. Sometimes, however, they will open them to journalists for the publicity. Still, it is nice to know that someone is living that way, isn't it?

Nearly all of the major hotels have health spas available to both men and women, and those listed above, along with the Las Vegas Hilton, are quite lavish. Of course, all major hotels also have beauty salons, barbershops, and shopping arcades—some even featuring furriers.

Here is a selection of hotels that are considered the most fun places in Las Vegas. *Deluxe,* $60 a day and up; *Expensive,* $50–$60; *Moderate,* $40–$50; *Inexpensive,* under $40.

Bally's Las Vegas, 3645 Las Vegas Blvd. S. (739-4111). Formerly the MGM Grand, this hotel has often been called "a city within a city," because it is the only hotel in the city with two full-size show rooms, an international celebrity in one, a $10-million production show in the other. With 2,832 rooms and suites, it is one of the world's largest luxury hotels. It has seven restaurants, and arcade of 40 shops, the most unusual movie theater in the city, and the largest and most beautiful casino in Las Vegas. *Deluxe.*

Caesars Palace, 3570 Las Vegas Blvd. S. (731–7110). A veritable palace, indeed. Architecturally sumptuous, Caesars Palace is a delight to the eye both day and night. While the casino is on the smallish size compared to Bally's across the street, Caesars is a delight just to wander through.

See the 20-foot-high statute of David, carved with marble from the same quarry Michelangelo used. See Cleopatra's Barge, which gently rocks back and forth while you dance on it (inside the casino!). See the most expensive restaurant in Las Vegas, the Palace Court, in a setting of trees, shrubs, and flowers. Enjoy a Roman feast in the Bacchanal, where you are served by beautiful handmaidens. (Don't touch; they belong to Caesar.) Thrill to the futuristic Omnimax Theater. Caesars is everything a truly expensive vacation should be. *Deluxe.*

Desert Inn, 3145 Las Vegas Blvd. S. (733–4444). Once the home of Howard Hughes, who lived on the top floor, who owned the Frontier across the street from his room, and who was almost never seen by anyone. Hughes is gone now, but his hotel is just as wonderful as ever. The "D.I." has beautiful grounds and country club, and its golf course is said to be among the best. The Desert Inn is located right in the heart of the colorful Strip and has elevators running up the outside of the hotel. *Deluxe.*

Golden Nugget, 129 E. Fremont St. (385–7111). The only truly luxury hotel in the downtown area, it was developed by that wunderkind of the casino-hotel world, Steve Wynn. Luxurious decor, one of the most attractive casinos, fine restaurants, and the most extravagant high-roller suites in Las Vegas. (They go for more than $1,000 a day but usually are given away.) Wynn has brought a touch of elegance to the otherwise down-at-the-heels downtown area. With Sinatra and Willie Nelson now playing at the Golden Nugget rather than at Caesars, how could it be otherwise? *Deluxe.*

Union Plaza, 1 Main St. (386–2110). At the very best location in the heart of downtown: overlooking the neon wonderland of Fremont Street. Be sure to ask for a room in the front. In the back of the hotel is the new Amtrak station. The Union Plaza offers dinner-theater, which is an excellent buy. A Broadway play or musical is offered with semi-stars. *Expensive.*

A secret about inexpensive rooms: The only slow period of the year in Las Vegas is during the last 2 weeks before Christmas, when the city slows to a crawl, many of the shows are closed, and some executives even go on a vacation.

If you would like to go there then, you can almost name your price for a hotel room. Many of the hotels offer special deals for rooms, but often they are not publicized for prestige reasons. Two of the best pre-Christmas deals in town are at the *Hacienda Hotel,* at the far end of the Strip, and at the *Stardust,* right in the heart of the Strip. Would you believe $7.50 for a Strip hotel room? Don't tell them that we told you.

Sam's Town, 5111 Boulder Hwy. (456–7777). This hotel and old-time gambling hall is a little out of the way, not near either the Strip or the downtown. Still, it is very popular with people who like an informal setting, cheaper prices, and a cowboy atmosphere. Very colorful, a lot of down-home fun, popular with the locals, a huge Western Emporium right next to it, and two unusually good restaurants: Diamond Lil's and Willy and Jose's (Mexican). *Moderate.*

HOTELS AND MOTELS

Dunes, 3650 Las Vegas Blvd. S. (737–4110). Across from Caesars Palace and Bally's. An institution and an attractive hotel. The restaurant on the 26th floor has one of the best views to be found anywhere in the city, and you can go up there for dancing, as well. On the grounds, a fine golf course. *Deluxe.*

Las Vegas Hilton, 3000 Paradise Rd., next to the convention center (732–5111). The world's largest luxury resort hotel, with more than 3,000 rooms. Eleven restaurants, some of them surrounding an indoor rainfall. Everything that you expect a Hilton Hotel to be—and then some. Convenient to the convention center but not convenient to the Strip; you'll need a cab. *Deluxe.*

Riviera, 2901 Las Vegas Blvd. S. (734–5110). One of the oldest and most reliable names in Las Vegas. Superstar entertainment and fine restaurants. Nice grounds. Owned by Pia Zadora's hubby (some of the profits went to finance her career). *Deluxe.*

Alexis Park, 375 E. Harmon Ave. (796–3300). Las Vegas' newest hotel and the only one without a casino or slot machines. They planned it that way. For people who want elegance without all the casino trappings, this is a resort hotel of the first order. *Expensive.*

Flamingo Hilton, 3555 Las Vegas Blvd. S. (733–3111). The site of the very first luxury hotel in Las Vegas, built by gangster Bugsy Siegel shortly after World War II. The hotel was a bust then, but it has become very successful under the Hilton umbrella. If you want to be in a Hilton Hotel in the center of all of the action, this is the place. Incidentally, Bugsy's rose garden is still out back of the hotel . . . somewhere. *Expensive.*

Frontier, 3120 Las Vegas Blvd. S. (734–0110). In the very heart of the Strip (formerly owned by Howard Hughes) and home to one of the best shows on the Strip: superstar magicians Siegfried & Roy in "Beyond Belief." More wild animals than you have seen outside of a circus. If you like the slots, this is a good hotel for you to stay at. *Expensive.*

Imperial Palace, 3535 Las Vegas Blvd. S. (731–3311). Next to the Flamingo Hilton. Has a most attractive casino. It's the only hotel in the city with an oriental decor. Good location. *Expensive.*

Sahara, 2535 Las Vegas Blvd. S. (737–2111). Another old, reliable name. The home of Don Rickles and neighbor to the new Wet 'n' Wild waterpark. *Expensive.*

Sands, 3355 Las Vegas Blvd. S. (733–5000). Once home of the Sinatra-Martin "Rat Pack" of the fifties. Unusual architecture—a round hotel. A nice place to stay, but not what it was back then. Very convenient location on the Strip. *Expensive.*

Tropicana, 3801 Las Vegas Blvd. S. (739–2222). Nearest major hotel to the airport. The "Trop" was always a nice hotel, but it has recently added some spectacular landscaping. Has an attractive casino and is home of the American version of "Folies Bergère." A beautiful golf course. Altogether, a nice hotel. *Expensive.*

Binion's, 128 Fremont St., downtown (382–1600). The one hotel in Las Vegas where the sky is the limit when it comes to gambling. A man once walked in with a suitcase containing $250,000 in cash, and after placing one bet on roulette, he walked out with a half-million. The IRS reportedly is still hunting for him. The gambling here can be quite exciting. *Moderate.*

Circus Circus, 2880 Las Vegas Blvd. S. (734–0410). If you are bringing the kids and want to have fun, this is the one hotel in Las Vegas to bring them to, for it is the only hotel on the Strip that caters to families with children. The mezzanine above the gambling casino is like a circus midway, with every children's game known to man. In addition, live circus acts perform free day and night. The kids love it—and they can look over the railing and watch their parents lose money (children are not allowed onto the casino floor). W. C. Fields would have *hated* the place. *Moderate.*

Four Queens, 202 E. Fremont St., downtown (385–4011). Attractive hotel. All rooms are the same price. Home of Alan Grant's nationally broadcast "Jazz in Las Vegas" on Monday nights. *Moderate.*

Hacienda, 3950 Las Vegas Blvd. S. (739–8911). At the far end of the Strip. Recently refurbished, this hotel has always been a good buy because of its somewhat remote location. It's even better now. Offers an ice show. *Moderate.*

Holiday Inn, 3475 Las Vegas Blvd. S. (369–5000). In the very heart of the Strip, this hotel is immensely popular as a good value, and the casino is even popular with the locals. It has the reputation of being "loose." A colorful hotel for a Holiday Inn, and the buffets are among the best values in town. Just ask any local. They go there all the time. *Moderate.*

Landmark, 364 Convention Center Dr. (733–1110). Across from the convention center and the Las Vegas Hilton. The hotel with the most unusual architecture in the city. You can't miss it; the Landmark looks like a mushroom. The casino and the food are just so-so, but its rooftop drinking-and-dining establishment has a striking view of the city. The pool, which also is very attractive, was used in a James Bond movie. (The girl was tossed out the window of one hotel, fell past another, and landed in the pool of the Landmark, a feat that only Hollywood could pull off.) *Moderate.*

Maxim, 160 E. Flamingo St. (731–4300). A relatively small but well-appointed hotel with an attractive casino. It's chief virtue lies in being right across the street from the huge Bally's Las Vegas. In case you cannot get in there, the Maxim is a good second choice. *Moderate.*

Showboat, 2800 E. Fremont St. (385–9123). In an out-of-the-way location that is near neither the Strip nor the downtown. Still, the Showboat is very popular with families, probably because of its relatively low prices and the fact that it houses the biggest bowling alley of any hotel in Las Vegas (108 lanes). *Moderate.*

Stardust, 3000 Las Vegas Blvd. S. (732–6111). In the very center of the Strip. Good value for the money, even though it is one of the older hotels. Home of America's "Lido de Paris." *Moderate.*

GREAT VALUES

The Las Vegas area abounds in motels, but one of the best values for the money is the **Bali Hai,** 336 E. Desert Inn Rd. (734–2141), located only half a block from the very heart of the Strip. Very comfortable rooms, some with a kitchen; nice grounds; pleasant pool. Moderately priced. Here is a selection of others, all in the *Moderate* price range:

Airport Inn, 5100 Paradise Rd. (798–2777). Very close to the airport.

Ambassador Inn, 377 E. Flamingo Rd. (733–7777). Between the airport and the Strip; attractive.

Highlander Inn, 211 E. Flamingo Rd. (733–7800). Near Bally's.

Imperial Inn, 3265 Las Vegas Blvd. S. (735–5102). At the center of the Strip.

Mardi Gras, 3500 Paradise Rd. (731–2020). All rooms are mini-suites.

Mini-Price, 4155 Koval Lane (731–2111). Behind Bally's.

Mirage, 4613 Las Vegas Blvd. S. (739–6636). Features a beautiful pool with windows.

Rodeway Inn, 3786 Las Vegas Blvd. S. (736–1434). Convenient location and quieter than most.

Somerset House, 294 Convention Center Dr. (735–4411). Near the Strip and the convention center.

Tam o' Shanter, 3317 Las Vegas Blvd. S. (735–7331). Near the Circus Circus Hotel.

TraveLodge, 3419 Las Vegas Blvd. S. (734–6801). At the center of the Strip.

Vagabond Inn, 3688 Las Vegas Blvd. S. (736–0991). Next to the Dunes Hotel.

Westward Ho, 2900 Las Vegas Blvd. S. (731–2900). Center of the Strip; more than 1,000 rooms.

FOR TIGHT BUDGETS

If you've lost your wad in the casinos, here are a few hotels in the *Inexpensive* range:

City Center, 700 E. Fremont St., downtown (382–4766).

El Cid, 233 S. 6th St., near downtown (384–4696).

Golden Inn, 120 Las Vegas Blvd. N., downtown (384–8204).

Marianna Inn, 1322 E. Fremont St., near downtown (385–1150).

Motel 6, 195 E. Tropicana Ave., near the Tropicana Hotel (736–4904).

Travel Inn, 217 Las Vegas Blvd. N., downtown (384–3040).

Dining

The many diverse places to eat in Las Vegas range all the way from lavish and expensive hotel restaurants that will provide you with a dining experience you will remember for the rest of your life to small, memorable, out-of-the-way places, and all the way back up to one of the great dining bargains in America: Las Vegas hotel buffets.

Here is a sampling of places to eat in Las Vegas. *Expensive*, more than $25 a person; *Moderate*, $15 to $20; *Inexpensive*, under $15.

Our choice of the three best restaurants in Las Vegas (your selections may differ) includes the **Palace Court,** Caesars Palace, 3570 Las Vegas Blvd. S. (731–7547), nestled in a beautiful and sumptuous setting of trees, shrubs, and flowers. The roof rolls back to reveal the sky when the weather is good. An elegant setting, with gold plates and cutlery and cut crystal. The food, classically French, matches the setting. An evening of pure enchantment. Figure on about $100 for two for a meal worth remembering.

Andre's, 401 S. 6th St. (385–5016). This restaurant is in an odd location: in a private home near the downtown. A little hard to get to, but the local cognoscenti consider it to be the best restaurant in the city. Classic French, winner of the *Holiday* magazine award. *Expensive.*

Our other choice is **Gigi's,** Bally's, 3645 Las Vegas Blvd. S. (739–4111). The room is patterned after one at the famed Palace of Versailles, and some of the furnishings were even used in the movie *Marie Antoinette.* The fare is classic French, and the service is impeccable. Plan on paying about $80 for two.

HOTEL DINING ROOMS

If you have a little money and want to have a good, romantic time at a hotel gourmet dining room, Las Vegas is an ideal place to do it. The sophistication of the city has grown a lot since the only dining to be found was at the hotel "chuckwagons." Besides the two already mentioned, here is a selection of gourmet dining rooms, all in the *Expensive* category:

Benihana Village, Las Vegas Hilton (732–5111). Heralded as a "Japanese fantasyland come to life," Benihana is the only complex of its kind in the world and has to be seen to be believed. Five stunning restaurants surround lush gardens and running streams.

Delmonico's, Riveria Hotel (735–5514). A quiet, sophisticated place in the midst of casino turmoil. Try the Tournedos Rossini.

Dome of the Sea, Dunes Hotel (737–4110). Another fine seafood restaurant. While you eat, a mermaid floats around playing a harp. Oh well, what else is new?

Lillie Langtry, Golden Nugget (385–7111). One of the earliest and best Chinese restaurants in the city.

Michael's, Barbary Coast (737–7111). An excellent steak and seafood house.

Top of the Mint, Mint Hotel (387–MINT). Elegant dining and dancing with a great view of the downtown lights.

SOME FUN PLACES TO EAT

If you want to get away from elegant restaurants and posh hotel dining rooms, here is a selection of places to eat where the emphasis is on fun. Most are small restaurants, but all are popular with both Las Vegans and visitors.

Aristocrat, 850 S. Rancho Dr., in the Towne and Country Center (870–1977). Las Vegans have twice voted this delightful place their favorite gourmet restaurant. *Expensive.*

Bacchanal, Caesars Palace, 3570 Las Vegas Blvd. S. (731–7525). It's like a Roman orgy! Well, not really. There are some restraints, you know. But when a fellow is sitting there enjoying an expensive Roman feast and a beautiful toga-clad "slave girl" is massaging the back of his neck, he might feel like it's the beginning of any orgy. Sexist? Certainly, but women are invited, too. *Expensive.*

Pamplemousse, 400 E. Sahara (733–2066). Given its name because the late Bobby Darin, a close friend of the owner, thought that the word *pamplemousse* (grapefruit) was the most beautiful in the French language. Aside from that, this is one of the most beautiful and one of the best small restaurants in Las Vegas. They even will prepare special dishes for you on short notice. *Expensive.*

Alpine Village Rathskeller, 3003 Paradise Rd. (734 –6888). The ratskeller is downstairs from the Alpine Village restaurant. With an oom-pah-pah band and people rollicking and singing, it's almost like Oktoberfest in Munich. A lot of fun and good German-Swiss food. *Moderate.*

Battista's, 4041 Audrie, right across from Bally's (732–1424). More fun than a barrel of opera singers. Battista Locatelli, a former opera singer dedicated to the highest quality in Italian food, opened a little restaurant called Hole in the Wall some years ago. Then the big MGM Grand moved in across the street, and—mama mia!—Battista's became a big success. The menu is often interrupted by the sound of opera. *Moderate.*

Cafe Michelle, 1350 E. Flamingo Rd. (735–8686). Would you believe a genuine French cafe with outdoor tables in the heart of Las Vegas? Cafe Michelle filled a need and has been a success from the day it opened. Good French food; very popular with locals. *Moderate.*

Cosmos, 32 E. Fremont St. (382–0330). Where else but in Las Vegas would you find an underground restaurant with trees growing in it? Attractive, large, excellent Italian food, in the heart of the downtown. *Moderate.*

Huey's, 2600 E. Flamingo Rd. (732–8411). This little neighborhood place was so popular that it built new and bigger quarters. Good drinks and food, mostly Mexican. Great hamburgers. *Moderate.*

Marrakech, 4632 S. Maryland Pkwy. (736–7655), across from the university. The only Moroccan restaurant in the city. Actually, some say it's the best restaurant of *any* kind in the city. At any rate, it's a lot of fun and you sit on the floor to eat, while watching the belly dancers. *Moderate.*

Old Heidelberg, 604 E. Sahara (731–5310). Also near the Sahara Hotel. A small, attractive German restaurant and shop with friendly personnel and wonderful German food. Try the homemade sausages. *Moderate.*

Play It Again, Sam, 4120 Spring Mountain Rd. (876–1550). If you have wanted to play Humphrey Bogart at least once in your life—to be able to sit there and say with conviction, "Here's lookin' at you, kid"—then this is the place to do it. Play It Again, Sam looks like a restaurant you might find in Morocco; it looks like—well, it looks like Rick's in *Casablanca,* complete with the slowly circling fans overhead. There's also a guy playing the piano, and while his name may not be Sam, we'll bet he can play "As Time Goes By." The food is pretty good, too. *Moderate.*

Ricardo's, 2380 E. Tropicana Ave. (798–4515). Our choice as the best Mexican restaurant in the city—and there are a lot of them. A big, popular place, with a strolling mariachi band. Wonderful margaritas and excellent food. A good place if you're in a group; they can handle crowds. *Moderate.*

Tillerman, 2245 E. Flamingo Rd. (731–4036). The Tillerman has been a part of the Las Vegas scene for some time now, and its reputation is growing. The reason: consistently good food and friendly, efficient service. An attractive restaurant, with excellent seafood and steaks and good drinks. *Moderate.*

Chicago Joe's, 820 S. 4th St. (382–5246). A little hard to get to, but worth the trouble. This tiny restaurant has been around a long time. Reason? Excellent Italian food. *Inexpensive.*

OTHER RESTAURANTS

It was not too long ago that Las Vegas was just a one-rattlesnake town. Those times have changed for good. Today, Las Vegas has a wealth of restaurants and can offer a wide variety of cuisines. Here are some of our other suggestions, listed by classification:

AMERICAN

Cattleman's Steak House, 2635 S. Maryland Pkwy. (732–7726). A Las Vegas institution. Good value for the money. *Moderate.*

Flite Deck, 6005 Las Vegas Blvd. S., in the Hughes Executive Terminal (739–1117). Dine while the planes from nearby McCarran International Airport whoosh overhead. A nice spot, but a bit noisy. *Moderate.*

Golden Steer, 308 W. Sahara (384–4470). Near the

Strip and the Sahara Hotel. A Las Vegas institution. May be the best steaks in town. *Moderate.*

Vince's, 4213 W. Sahara (876–5698). You'll need a cab to get to this one, but it's worth it. Excellent food and service. *Moderate.*

CHINESE

Chin's, 2300 E. Desert Inn (733–7764). Many have pronounced this attractive place to be the best Chinese restaurant in the city. Popular with the beautiful people. *Moderate.*

Silver Dragon, 1501 E. Flamingo Rd. (737–1234). A beautiful restaurant with unusual cuisine. *Moderate.*

GERMAN

Alpine Village, 3003 Paradise Rd. (734–6888). Across the street from the Las Vegas Hilton. Beautiful restaurant, excellent German-Austrian food. Also a lively rathskeller. *Expensive.*

ITALIAN

Bootlegger, 5025 S. Eastern (736–4939). An excellent reputation with the locals. *Moderate.*

Chateau Vegas, 565 E. Desert Inn (733–8282). Across the street from the convention center. This place used to have the reputation of being the best in town. Now, there are a lot more places, but it is still not far from the best. *Moderate.*

Gianni Russo's State Street, 2570 State St. (733–0225). Gianni Russo was in the movie *The Godfather,* and both he and his attractive restaurant are very popular with celebrities. A plus is Gianni's singing. *Moderate.*

Limelight, 2340 E. Tropicana Ave. (739–1410). A new and attractive restaurant gaining a good reputation. *Moderate.*

Mariano's, 3513 S. Valley View Rd. (871–4596). Not far from the Strip. A beautiful new restaurant with excellent food and a piano player at night. *Moderate.*

The Olive Garden, 1545 E. Flamingo Rd. (735–0082). Rapidly becoming the in place with the wealthy local professionals. Attractive restaurant with a pleasant atmosphere.

Venetian, 3713 W. Sahara (876–4190). Another Las Vegas institution, very popular with the locals. *Moderate.*

Vineyard, 3630 S. Maryland Pkwy. (731–1606). This restaurant has always been very popular with college students because of its good food at reasonable prices. Also, the best salad bar in town. *Moderate to Inexpensive.*

JAPANESE

Ginza, 1000 E. Sahara Ave. (732–3080). Attractive little restaurant; unusual menu. *Moderate.*

Osaka, 4205 W. Sahara Ave. (876–4988). A little out of the way, but worth it. *Moderate.*

MEXICAN

Viva Zapata, 3540 W. Sahara Ave. (873–7228). This one has been around a long time, and for good reason. *Moderate.*

El Burrito, 1919 E. Fremont St. (387–9246). Near the Showboat Hotel. This hole-in-the-wall has been there forever and never grown any larger, but the locals swear by it. *Inexpensive.*

VIETNAMESE

Saigon, 4251 W. Sahara Ave. (362–9978). For those who want to experience a still-unfamiliar cuisine that is finding favor in the United States. *Moderate.*

SEAFOOD

Lobster Trap, 953 E. Sahara, in the Commercial Center (734–0023). This place is comfortable and unpretentious. Just good, fresh seafood. *Moderate.*

ROOMS WITH A VIEW

Center Stage, Union Plaza Hotel, 1 Main St. (386–2512). A new restaurant built on top of an old swimming pool with the best view of the brightly lighted downtown to be had anywhere. *Moderate.*

Top of the Landmark, 364 Convention Center Dr. (733–1110). The food here is just so-so, but the view is panoramic. This is also a fine place for dancing at night. *Moderate.*

Top of the Mint, Mint Hotel, 100 E. Fremont St. (385–7440). An elevator goes up the outside of the hotel to the restaurant and affords you an excellent view of the downtown area. *Moderate.*

Tracy's, Bally's Las Vegas, 3645 Las Vegas Blvd. S. (739–4930). Don't be fooled by the name. This is one of the best Chinese restaurants in the city. Large and attractive, with a view of the Strip. *Moderate.*

FAST FOODS

For a savory pizza, try **Battista's,** 1041 Audrie, across from **Bally's** (733–3950). Battista Locatelli wanted to make the best pizza in Las Vegas, so he opened this little place next to his Hole-in-the-Wall restaurant. It *is* the best.

A juicy, tasty cheeseburger can be had at **Marie Cal-**

lender's, 600 E. Sahara Ave. and 4800 S. Eastern Ave. They also serve delicious pies. According to the *Review Journal* newspaper, the best hamburgers in town are at **Flaky Jake's,** 2870 S. Maryland Pkwy. (794–0900).

BUFFETS

The hotel buffets are, bar none, the best dining bargains to be found in Las Vegas. All of the major hotels have them, and they average $2 for breakfast, $3 for lunch, and $4–$6 for dinner. They include things like roast beef, baked ham, fried chicken, etc. And, of course, it's usually "all you can eat."

Some of the most notable hotel buffets may be found at the **Dunes,** particularly during a weekend champagne brunch, the **Tropicana, Caesars Palace,** the **Flamingo Hilton,** the **Sands,** the **Sahara,** the **Las Vegas Hilton,** and the **Mint,** in the downtown area. Following is a select list of hotels where you may expect to find fine buffet dining:

Try **Caesars Palace** for Sunday brunch. One of Las Vegas' most sumptuous buffets, as you would expect at this hotel. Adults, $9.50, children $8.50.

Just about the largest buffet in the city in terms of the number of things to eat can be had at **Circus Circus.** Breakfast, $2.29; brunch, $2.49; dinner, $3.49.

Fremont is very popular with both visitors and locals. Breakfast, $2.95; lunch, $3.50; dinner, $4.95.

Frontier, also quite logically, features a "Chuckwagon Buffet." Breakfast or lunch, $3.95; includes champagne.

Golden Nugget advertises it has one of the best buffets in town, according to the mother of the hotel's president, who appears in commercials with him. Breakfast, $4; lunch, $7; dinner, $8.50. Sunday champagne brunch, $8.50.

"El Gran Buffet" at **Hacienda** (where else?) is popular with locals as well as visitors. Breakfast, $3.95; lunch, $3.95; dinner, $4.95. Sunday champagne brunch, $4.95.

One of the most popular buffets in town, and certainly one of the great bargains, is at **Holiday Casino.** Breakfast, $2.57; lunch, $2.57; dinner, $3.57. You can't even eat at home for those prices!

"Emperor's Buffet" at **Imperial Palace** boasts a great variety of delicious food. Breakfast or lunch, $2.99; dinner, $3.99; Saturday and Sunday champagne brunch, $6.50.

Enjoy a buffet beside a very attractive hotel pool (and waterfall!) in the Cascade Terrace at the **Landmark Hotel.** Breakfast, $3.48; lunch, $4.48; dinner, $5.98. The hotel also has a Sunday brunch on the 27th floor with a great view of the city. Adults, $7.95; children, $3.50.

Palace Station also has a Sunday champagne brunch —new, but a really good one; also offers some pasta specialties from its Pasta Palace restaurant. $4.95—and that includes champagne!

In the tradition of its culinary excellence, the **Riviera** features a "Gourmet Buffet." Breakfast, $1.95; lunch, $1.95; dinner with champagne, $3.95.

Sahara has cooked-to-order omelets and build-your-own sandwiches; complimentary wine with dinner. Breakfast $2.98; lunch, $3.75; dinner, $4.75. Saturday and Sunday brunch, $4.95.

A favorite with the locals is the **Showboat.** Breakfast, $2.95; lunch, $4.25; dinner, $5.95. Saturday and Sunday champagne brunch, $4.25.

Silver Slipper is known for the abundance and variety of its display. Lunch, $3.95; dinner, $4.95.

Stardust also has a buffet with a huge selection. Daily brunch, $2.49; dinner, $3.49.

Sundance offers one of the most favored buffets in the downtown area. Breakfast, $1.99; lunch, $2.49; dinner, $3.75.

The "Island Buffet" at the **Tropicana** presents a colorful array of international foods that changes daily. Breakfast, $2.24; lunch, $2.49; dinner, $3.49.

Union Plaza dishes up a special weekend-only brunch served in the main show room with a variety of interesting dishes. $3.95, including champagne.

WHERE THE CABBIES EAT

If you're a stranger in Las Vegas, you might be tempted to ask a cabdriver, "Where's a good place to eat around here?"

Don't do it. A scam has been going on in Las Vegas for a couple of years that the city—without much success —has been trying to put a stop to. It goes like this: The drivers have a list of restaurants that will pay the driver a "bounty" for customers he brings there. Also, the restaurants are often as far away from the Strip as you can get and still be in the city. Consequently, the cab driver first gets a good fare out of his recommendation; then, when he has dropped you off in front of the restaurant, he drives around to the back and gets his payoff, usually $2–$5 a head.

A better source of information is people who work in the hotel where you are staying. Naturally, they are going to recommend the hotel restaurants first, but you can ask, "If I wanted to get out of the hotel, where would I go?" They live in Las Vegas, so they know where the good places are and often can steer you to an interesting out-of-the-way place that only the locals know.

A LATE-NIGHT SNACK

It is easier to get a late-night snack in Las Vegas than it is in most cities. All of the major hotels have at least one dining room that is open around the clock, usually the coffee shop, and many of the major hotels also have 24-hour room service. When you combine that with your ability to buy a drink any hour of the day or night, you should have no complaints.

If it's a full-course dinner you want, you will find these restaurants open throughout the night:

Chateau Vegas, 565 E. Desert Inn Rd. (733–8282). Gourmet.

Mariano's, 3513 S. Valley View Ave. (871–4596). Italian.

State Street, 2570 State St. (733–0225). Italian.

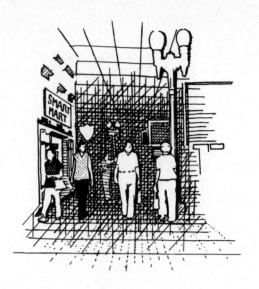

Shopping

Let's say you just made a heavy win at one of the casino's gaming tables and all that money is burning a hole in your purse or wallet. You want to run out on a shopping spree for gifts for yourself or that certain someone. Las Vegas has an array of smart shops and boutiques to help you part with that newly won money.

The swankiest shops can be found in the **Fashion Show Mall** (369–8382), on the Strip at Spring Mountain Rd., right next to the Frontier Hotel. First stop here should be *Miller Stockman,* purveyors of Western wear, for hip-length sheepskin coats and cowboy hats. As a counterbalance, *Princess Vera-Nocce* offers drop-dead, slinky dresses that would make any woman the hit of a party.

The white fox fur at *Marshall Rousso's* may be a little too expensive, but the snakeskin boots are a little more affordable. Or you might consider a black sheath dress at *Neiman Marcus.*

For men, the *Style Center* lives up to its name with the latest fashion accessories, including Indiana Jones-style hats. For the fanciful, there are charming crystal figures at the *Crystal Palace.*

If your tastes are more on the serious side, stop in

at the *American Museum of Historical Documents,* where you can pick up authentic letters, such as one from Mark Twain or Marilyn Monroe. Letters are framed, dated, and include a picture of the author.

If your packages are getting heavy now, you can stop in *El Portal* and consider the mechanical Omnibot robot to help you carry them. Nearby are *Midnight Lace* and *Victoria's Secrets,* where you may find that pegnoir or teddy bear you've been looking for.

All sorts of leisure-time gifts, including an ivory backgammon set, are available at *Abercrombie & Fitch.* You can pick up some bubble bath at *Crabtree & Evelyn,* purveyors of fine English toiletry products, for a relaxing bath back at the hotel.

You can finish your shopping spree at the mall with some leisurely browsing through *Minotaur,* the finest art gallery in Las Vegas.

After a quick, refreshing ice-cream soda at *Haagen-Daz,* hop in a cab to **Caesars Palace,** which is only two blocks away. The Palace's shopping arcade is small, but well represented in exclusive shops.

The arcade includes *Gucci,* whose perfume is very popular. You can browse through *Cartier*'s array of fine watches and jewelry, and *Ted Lapidus,* which stocks a "Miami Vice"-type jacket for men. Also located in this arcade is *Galerie St. Tropez,* which features some of Leroy Neiman's paintings.

Right across the street from Caesars Palace is **Bally's Las Vegas,** which has the largest shopping arcade (40 shops) of any hotel in the city. *Country Palace* sells Christmas-tree decorations and country-style crafts. Consider a single string of pearls at *Le Grand Jewels,* and the stunning doeskin swimsuits and at the *French Room.* For a bit of whimsy, as well as a souvenir of your stay in Las Vegas, you can stop in at the *Movie Set Photo Studio* to have your picture taken in costume. You can choose from a riverboat gambler to a turn-of-the-century chorus girl costumes. If it's pictures of real stars you're looking for, you'll find them at the *Nostalgia Shop,* which is devoted to the history of movies. They have everything there, including the poster of James Dean in *Giant.*

As you prepare to leave the arcade, finally tired out

from all that shopping, you notice that the Bally's Movie Theater is showing one of your old favorites, such as *Casablanca.* So go in, relax, and watch the movie in all the luxury and comfort of a Hollywood screening room. It's been a busy shopping day and you deserve a rest.

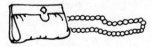

All the other major hotels also offer expensive shopping arcades and stores to supply you with those items you forgot to pack or ran out of. Two other malls are worth mention:

Meadows Mall, 4300 Meadows Lane (878–4849), is an attractive place, with more than 140 stores, several miles from the Strip.

Boulevard Mall, 3528 S. Maryland Pkwy. (735–8268), is just 2 miles from the Strip and has 110 stores.

If you are looking for something unusual, either for yourself or for giving, you're apt to find it in these shops:

Partout, 3355 Spring Mountain Rd. (362–9330), is not far from the Strip. High-quality gifts from around the world.

Western Emporium, next to Sam's Town Hotel and Gambling Hall (454–8017), is a huge store full of Western gifts, clothing, boots, and other imported items from around the world, as well as a gourmet shop.

Souvenirs of Las Vegas and the Southwest are available at *Souvenir & Gift World,* 3065 Las Vegas Blvd. S. (737–1209); *Las Vegas Souvenirs & Gifts,* 312 E. Fremont St., downtown (385–2736); and *Discount Souvenirs & Gifts,* 3269 Las Vegas Blvd. S. (369–7364).

Indian handicrafts and jewelry can be found at *The Tepee,* Bally's Las Vegas Hotel Shopping Arcade, 3645 Las Vegas Blvd. (735–5333); *Turquoise Chief,* 1408 Las Vegas Blvd. S. (385–7011); and *West of Dallas,* in the **Fashion Show Mall** on the Strip at Spring Mountain Rd. (737–3375).

Casinos

Las Vegas casinos are some of the largest and most beautiful in the world. The biggest one (50,000 square feet), and probably the most elegant, with high ceilings and 60 crystal chandeliers, is at Bally's Las Vegas. Some other attractive casinos are at the Golden Nugget (downtown), the Tropicana Hotel, the Imperial Palace Hotel, and Caesars Palace.

Nearly all of the hotel casinos are open 24 hours a day. You have to be at least 21 to play. Those under 21 are not allowed in the casino, but in most of the hotels, there are convenient areas where they can look over a railing and watch their parents lose money—and wonder why.

Photography is not allowed in the casino. This is very annoying to guests who would like to have their picture taken in front of a slot machine, but that's the way it is. Contrary to what some people think, the ban is not a law but rather a hotel policy, and the reason for it is to protect the privacy of guests and not to disturb the gamers. You get the picture.

The only exception to this rule is if you have just won a lot of money (usually, over $25,000) at one of the games. In that case, the hotel may wish to have a picture taken of you to use for publicity purposes. Also, when the win is high, the casino is required to take a Polaroid picture of you for the benefit of the IRS. (When a restaurant worker from Milwaukee won almost $1 million on a progressive dollar slot machine at the MGM Grand, the hotel certainly wanted to take a picture of him.)

While hotels such as Caesars Palace and Bally's were not built by sending people home with more money than they brought, it does sometimes happen, and wins of $250,000 are not uncommon. Wins of less than that occur all the time, of course, and even you may get lucky.

Do you get all of the money? To the surprise of many people, you do. If you win $500,000 at a progressive slot machine, for instance, the hotel will first identify you via a Social Security card and a picture identification; then they take the Polaroid picture; and finally, they give you a check for the entire amount. It is up to you and the IRS to settle what you owe Uncle Sam.

Of course, you *could* always head for the nearest travel agent.

Seriously, one tip on a big win: See your accountant about income averaging.

The $250,000 wins occur at the major hotels about six times a year, but smaller wins occur all the time.

If you spend any time gambling, you will find that you are constantly being offered free drinks of your choice. How can the hotel do this, you wonder. Aren't they losing money? Don't worry about it—they aren't losing money.

Free drinks may be fun if you are dealing with something as simple as a one-armed bandit. But they may be less fun if you are in a more complicated game, such as poker or craps. The free drink you want there may be only club soda or coffee.

Games offered in the casinos:

Baccarat is the game of James Bond, the class game

of Las Vegas. All you have to do is take a look at the baccarat pit to realize this. A lot of money goes down in this game. No skill at all is involved, and it's easy to learn. The game is pure chance, which some gamers love, and the stakes can often be quite high.

Bingo is featured in some hotels. But if you're going to come to Las Vegas only to play bingo, why bother to leave home?

Blackjack is easy to play and fun. It's one game where the odds can even be slightly in your favor if you are a good card counter and know when a face card is likely to come up. But that's a lot of work and only for the professional. For the rest of us, blackjack, or 21, is fun and easy to learn.

You'll notice that blackjack dealers never smile. Perhaps it's because most of them made only $50,000 to $100,000 last year, and the government says they have to declare their tokes, which the dealers say they never got.

Craps is a complicated dice game requiring skill and knowledge. It used to be learned growing up on the streets or in the army, but now, more and more craps tables are being replaced with slot machines. Still, craps is a really exciting game when it is hot. Listen to all that shouting!

Keno. You just pick a couple of numbers you like, mark them on a slip of paper, and give them to a keno runner with a couple of dollars. The odds are not real good in keno and it's time-consuming, but it is fun, and you can win up to $50,000 for just a few bucks.

Poker. People who are dedicated to this game are *really* dedicated, and it is not uncommon for them to play around the clock in tournaments. It's fun to watch as well as play. The annual poker tournament at Binion's Horseshoe, downtown, draws huge crowds.

Roulette is another international game that is fairly easy to learn and a lot of fun. You'll think you're at the casino in Monte Carlo when you get rolling with roulette. Incidentally, a lot of European gamers are surprised to discover how noisy Las Vegas casinos are. The European casinos contain only three games—baccarat, 21, and roulette—and they are a lot quieter. No slot machines. More conservative. Not as much fun.

Slot machines are increasing in popularity all the time. All you need is one good arm to learn how to play them. In recent years, progressive slot machines have become more and more popular. With the aid of a computer, the jackpot on progressive slots keeps going up and up until someone wins it. You can win as much as $1 million on a progressive dollar machine, as much as $250,000 on a quarter machine, and as much as $25,000 on a nickel machine! Also increasing in popularity are the video slots, where everything is displayed on a video screen. The random selection is supposed to be the same as on a regular machine. Some people prefer playing video poker or blackjack, which also can be a lot of fun.

How to play the games

Baccarat. Wagers made in baccarat invariably are the highest in the casino, which adds to the excitement of this international "Game of James Bond." The game is played with eight decks of cards dealt from a "shoe." The object of the game is to have your cards total as close to 9 as possible. Face cards count as 10, and all others count at face value. Participants wager on one of two hands, either the player's or the bank's, each of whom is initially dealt two cards. The hand finally totaling 9 or the next closest to it is the winner. The last digit of the card total determines the hand value. For instance, two 9's total 18, so the value of the hand is 8. Two cards are dealt to the player having the largest wager against the bank and two cards to the person acting as banker. The player acts first. In case of a tie, the hand is played over.

Rules stipulate that when a third card is dealt, if the banker wins, he retains the shoe. When the banker loses, the shoe moves to the right, giving each player a chance to handle or pass the shoe. Many players like baccarat because it is a game where no real skill is involved; it's all pure luck. If you're feeling lucky that night, have a good bankroll, and like to sit next to well-dressed, often beautiful people, then go for it.

BLACKJACK

The object of the game is to draw cards that total as close to 21 as possible without exceeding it. Face cards count as 10, and the ace can count as either 1 or 11. The dealer gives each player two cards face down and gives himself two, one face up. The player may stand (take no more cards) or draw additional cards to try to get close to 21. If you bust (go over 21), you lose, even if the dealer also loses. If your total is closer to 21 than the dealer's, you win. If there is a tie, no one wins. Any ace with a ten, jack, queen, or king is automatically a blackjack (21). If both the player and the dealer have a blackjack, it's a tie.

Split bets: If the player's first two cards are of the same value, he may split them into two hands, betting the same amount on each.

Double down: A player can double his bet on any two cards and then draw one card only.

Insurance: If the dealer has an ace showing, a player make take insurance (bet up to one half of his original bet). If the dealer's down card is a ten, jack, queen, or king, the player wins two for one. If it is any other card, the dealer wins.

CRAPS

The most exciting and the noisiest game in the casino. Just look at all that action! Craps is a dice game in which every player has an opportunity to place a bet on *every* roll of the dice. If you bet the "pass line," you win on 7 or 11, and lose on 2, 3, or 12 on the first roll. If any other number comes up, it's your "point." If your point comes up again before 7 is thrown, you win; otherwise, you lose. If you bet on the "don't pass" line, you lose on 7 or 11 and win on 2 or 3 on the first roll. You also lose if the point comes up again before 7.

Come bet: A come bet may be made at any time after

the first roll. You win on 7 or 11; you lose on 2, 3, or 12. Any other number is your point. If your point comes up again before 7, you win.

Don't come: The reverse of a come bet. You lose on 7 or 11 and win on 2 or 3 (12 is a standoff). You win if 7 comes up before the point is made.

Field: A bet for one roll only. You bet on 2, 3, 4, 9, 10, 11, and 12. If any of these numbers is thrown on the next roll, you win even money except on 2 or 12, on which you win two-to-one.

Big 6 and 8: You win even money if 6 or 8 is rolled before 7.

Any 7: You win five-for-one if 7 is thrown on the first roll after your bet.

Hard ways: You win at odds quoted on the table layout if the exact combination of the numbers you bet comes up. You lose if the number is rolled any other way—or if 7 comes up.

Any craps: You win eight-for-one if 2, 3, or 12 is thrown on the first roll after your bet.

Eleven: You win fifteen-for-one if 11 is thrown on the first roll after your bet.

The odds: Once a point is established, either a shooter's point on the first roll or a come point on the succeeding roll, you can get odds with the dice or give odds against the dice. You get two-to-one on 10 and 4; three-to-two on 5 and 9; six-to-five on 8 and 6. You lay the same odds when you bet against the point.

Place bets: You may make a place bet on the following numbers: 4, 5, 6, 8, 9, and 10. The number you place must be made by the shooter before 7 is thrown.

KENO

The odds are not great in keno, but you can bet as little as $1 and win as much as $50,000. You get a slip with numbers on it from 1 to 80. Choose as few as one or as many as 15 numbers on the slip and give the slip and your bet to a keno runner or at the betting window. You will receive a duplicate ticket so you can compare it with the numbered board that will light up when the keno balls with numbers on them are randomly selected. Twenty winning numbers are selected for each game. For instance, if you had selected eight numbers at a typical casino and bet $5 and five of those numbers came up, you would win $45. If all eight of them came up, you would win $50,000!

ROULETTE

Roulette is a relatively easy game to learn. Take a look at the felt in front of you: You can place a bet on a single number (which pays the highest odds), on two numbers, by straddling the line, on three numbers, on four numbers, on the red or the black, on six numbers, etc. The more numbers you are covering with a single chip (or a stack of chips), the less you will win, of course, if you hit. When all the bets are down, as you have seen countless times in movies, the dealer will spin the little white ball in the roulette wheel, and where it stops is the winner. As we said, just study the felt for a few minutes, and that should tell you everything.

SLOTS

The slots are simplicity itself. Most of them are quite self-explanatory. Gamblers feel that you should bet the maximum number of coins each time. Your coins may be gone faster that way, but if you do win, you will win the maximum. A relatively recent innovation is the introduction of the video slot machine and the progressive carousel slots.

In these, a number of slot machines are linked together in a circle by computer so that each time someone plays one and loses, the total goes higher . . . and higher . . . and higher. You can win as much as a million dollars on one of the progressive dollar slot machines—and people have done it!

THE SLOT MACHINE IS KING

If you think there are more slot machines in the casinos every time you come to Las Vegas, you are absolutely right. The slot machine in its many variations is becoming king here. And there's a good reason for that.

In the old days, when Las Vegas was just getting off the ground—or off the desert—the slot machine was put in the casinos primarily to give a woman something to do while her husband or boyfriend was engaged in more "serious" gambling, such as craps, blackjack, or poker.

But as people became more sophisticated, fewer of them knew how to play the old, complicated games like craps. Consequently, the casinos have increasingly been moving the crap tables out in favor of slot machines.

But there is another reason: Slot machines have become more and more popular as they have delivered higher and higher payoffs. And the arrival of the video slot machines has increased their popularity even more.

But perhaps the biggest reason for the popularity of slots is that for $2 worth of nickels, you can have $2 worth of fun at a slot machine—even if you lose.

TIPS ON GAMBLING

Don't gamble when you are

- tired
- drunk
- angry
- losing.

Set a limit and stick to it.

EYE IN THE SKY

Look up. See all those mirrors in the ceiling of the casino? You're on "Candid Camera."

Those who have not been to Las Vegas before may never have heard of the "eye in the sky." The ceiling of every casino is a false dropped ceiling. Above the tables, in the ceiling, are two-way mirrors, and behind those mirrors are men on a dark catwalk watching the gaming. Of course, they trust *you*. Have you ever lied? Seriously, though, they trust you a lot more than they do their own dealers. If a dealer is in collusion with an outside party, the house can be taken for a lot of money. The thing that protects the house is the dealer's knowledge that he or she is being watched by eye, by binoculars, or by closed-circuit TV all the time. Incidentally, the eye-in-the-sky job has got to be the loneliest and most boring in Las Vegas—unless you're a real introvert.

Race and Sports Books. You don't have to go down to the corner cigar store anymore and say, "Louie sent me." You can bet on any sporting event or horse race, legally, right from your hotel. The most attractive race and sports book in town is at Caesars Palace, but other big ones may be found at the Stardust, the Fremont, and Bally's.

BEST ODDS

Real gamblers say the games with the best odds are blackjack, craps, and poker, and those with the worst odds are keno and the big wheel. Real gamblers also say the odds are better in the downtown area than on the Strip, and you can expect the worst odds of all where you have a captive audience, such as at the airport.

Does that mean that the slot machines can be changed to pay off more—or less? Yes, of course. There is nothing illegal about it; but the hotel has to be consistent in its payoff ratio.

Final tip: If a man approaches you and says he will bet you $100 he can make the joker jump out of the deck and spit in your eye, walk away. Unless, of course, you have a handkerchief handy and want to lose $100.

CHEATING IN LAS VEGAS?

The question most frequently asked by a first-time visitor to Las Vegas is whether gambling there is really honest.

Matter of fact, it is. It is made so by the Nevada Gaming Commission, which tightly regulates the casinos. It issues licenses and investigates such things as ownership of the casino. A casino would be in danger of losing its license if it tried to cheat its customers, and no casino is going to risk that for the sake of a few bucks more. There is too much to be made already.

In fact, the hotel-casino worries more about cheating by its own employees and by visitors (shame on you!).

You would not believe the ways people cheat. If they expended as much energy making an honest living, they probably would make a fortune.

They drop ice down the slot machine. They drill a little hole on the side. They put a coin on a piece of string. They use magnets. They use mirrors at the black-jack table. They work in collusion. They get foreign coins that are the same size as American coins of larger denomination. They make false keys. They . . . you get the picture.

Does any of this work? Well, do you think that the people who run Las Vegas are dummies?

HOW TO LOSE YOUR SHIRT

In the movie *Lost in America,* a California Yuppie couple who had just lost half their income by being fired decided to pull up stakes and go "look for America." They sold their house, pooled all their financial resources, bought a motor home, and took off. Their first stop was Las Vegas—where they gambled away every cent they had. The former advertising executive tried to convince the casino manager that if the hotel returned all his money it would show that "Las Vegas has a heart." He was not successful.

That makes a good movie, but in real life, it rarely happens. About the only way you could lose your entire life savings would be if you foolishly *brought* your entire life's savings with you, as this couple did. Otherwise, if you have lost a lot in Las Vegas but want to continue, do you think you will be able to cash a personal check? Do you think you can mortgage your home in Iowa, all the way from Las Vegas? As we have said, it hardly ever happens, despite the popular fantasy. Also, the hotels realize it would not look good.

But people do lose more money than they planned to in Las Vegas, of course. It happens all the time; just don't let one of the big losers be you.

ROYAL TREATMENT

There is no place in the world where the ordinary person can be so pampered as in Las Vegas—as long as that ordinary person—or couple—has some money and is willing to spend it.

But then, why not? You only live once, there is only one Las Vegas, and you can't take it with you. So why not spend it?

If you agree to the above, here is how you can live

like a king or queen in Las Vegas. . . or at least like a prince or princess.

When you arrive at McCarran International Airport, tip the skyhop generously and ask to be taken to the limousines. You will find several of them parked in front of the airport. The cost of a limo is $20 an hour.

But aren't limos there for high rollers? Of course they are, because high rollers have money. But if you can prove to the driver that you are willing to spend a little, you are on your way. Most Las Vegas hotels are relatively close to the airport, so it won't take long to get there.

Stay at one of the best luxury hotels. We suggest Caesars Palace, Bally's, or the Desert Inn. (You will have reserved well in advance, of course.) Bally's has 3,000 rooms, and every single room is occupied on Thursdays, Fridays, and Saturdays, so don't embarrass yourself by thinking you can get a room "when we get there."

Instead of just a room, arrange to get a suite. They cost a little more but are well worth it. Handle the reservation yourself, rather than using a travel agent, so you can find out what the hotel really has. Ask them to describe their suites so that you can discover what appeals to you. Bally's, for instance, has a celebrity suite that goes for $350 a day. It includes such things as a full wet bar, a large living room and dining area, an adjoining bedroom with large, canopied four-poster bed, two bathrooms, a sunken Roman tub with curtains around it, and a beautiful view of the city. Caesars Palace and the Golden Nugget also have a series of beautiful suites.

Tip the bellman generously (perhaps $20). This assures that he will be there when you want him and that he will be a good source of information for you. Bellmen seem to know more about the city and how to get what you want than anyone else.

Before going to dinner, quietly call the restaurant and ask for the name of the maître d'. If the maître d' is there, give your full name and explain that you and a guest are coming for dinner and say, "If you take care of me, I will take care of you." Maître d's know what this means.

Be sure to choose the very best restaurant you can

find. Most of the best are in the hotels. (See the *Restaurants* section.)

The maître d' who worked for many years at the lavish Queen Elizabeth buffet at the Dunes Hotel—his name was August—had it down to a science. Even if it was your first time there, he knew your name from the reservation, and the greeting would be effusively warm.

Then, he would look around in consternation and place his hand on his cheek, Jack Benny style. "*Every* table is taken or reserved." (He knows you can see empty tables.) "But for you, we will *always* have a table. Right this way."

You can imagine that August was always taken care of quite well.

Is this dishonest? Well maybe, but so what? The guest feels like royalty, his or her companion is impressed, and August is happy. You may think he does it only for the money, but he does not. "I like to make people happy," August says, and the way he says it, you know he is telling the truth.

The same routine works wonders with the maître d' at the show-room door. Call first, find out who he is, talk to him if you can, convince him that you are someone special and it would be worth his while to believe this— and he will take care of you.

Again, most of the best ones do it, believe it or not, because they enjoy seeing people happy as much as making money. Of course, money makes them happy, too.

One of the best show-room maître d's is Pete Bella at Bally's Celebrity Room. "I'm a sucker for old people and kids," he says. "I'll really go out of my way for them. If someone is nice to me, I'll be nice to them."

As explained earlier in the *General Information* section, Las Vegas is definitely not a place where the early bird gets the worm. You can arrive five minutes before show time and get one of the best seats in the house. How? Just tell the maître d' where you would like to sit, slip $50 into his hand, and you're on your way.

Finally, to cap off a perfect day, have some champagne and flowers sent up to your room.

Las Vegas is one city where dreams can come true.

Nightlife

Las Vegas calls itself "The Entertainment Capital of the World"—and with good reason. Just take a drive down the famed three-and-a-half-mile Strip. There are more entertainers here—and a greater variety of entertainment—than in any other city in the world.

THE SHOWS

There were reports a couple of years ago that the big entertainers didn't play Las Vegas any more, that they had all gone to Atlantic City. Don't believe it. For a short time, a few of the big hotels experimented with big production shows rather than an expensive star. But most have abandoned that idea now and have gone back to the S*U*P*E*R*S*T*A*R!

The reason is quite simple: When people return from Las Vegas, no one asks them, "What did you see?" They ask, "Who did you see?"

78

SUPERSTAR ENTERTAINMENT

Bally's Las Vegas, formerly the MGM Grand, at 3645 Las Vegas Blvd. S. (739–4567), has the best of both worlds. In the Celebrity Room, you'll find an array of superstars, including Dean Martin, Tom Jones, Sammy Davis, Jr., and Jerry Lewis. In the 1,100-seat Ziegfeld Theatre next door is a $10-million production show, *Jubilee!*, with a cast of hundreds.

Other showrooms that feature superstar entertainment are:

Las Vegas Hilton, 3000 Paradise Rd. (732–5755). Bill Cosby, Donna Summer, Wayne Newton, Engelbert Humperdinck.

Caesars Palace, 3570 Las Vegas Blvd. S. (731–7333). Joan Rivers, Donna Summer, Diana Ross, George Burns, Julio Iglesias, David Copperfield.

Golden Nugget, 129 Fremont St., downtown (386–3100). Frank Sinatra, Willie Nelson, David Brenner, Paul Anka.

Desert Inn, 3145 Las Vegas Blvd. S. (735–4566). Lynda Carter, Glen Cambell, Neil Sedaka.

Sahara, 2535 Las Vegas Blvd S. (737–2424). Don Rickles.

BIG PRODUCTION SHOWS

Bally's—*Jubilee!*, as noted above, which includes the Destruction of the Temple by Samson.

Frontier, 3120 Las Vegas Blvd. S. (734–0240). *Beyond Belief,* with magicians Siegfried and Roy and their menagerie of exotic animals. Easily one of the best shows in town; in their "family show" the magicians are fully clothed.

Tropicana, 3801 Las Vegas Blvd S. (739–2411). "Folies Bergere", an excellent recreation of the Paris act. Spectacular dances and sets.

Stardust, 3000 Las Vegas Blvd S. (732–6111). *Lido de Paris,* the import from Paris, with lots of beautiful, topless girls. Also features the hilarious Bobby Berosini and his orangutans.

SMALLER SHOWS

Flamingo Hilton, 3555 Las Vegas Blvd. S. (733–3333). *City Lites,* long-running ice extravaganza.

Hacienda, 3950 Las Vegas Blvd. S. (798–0571). *Minsky's Burlesque,* starring Irv Benson.

Holiday Casino, 3740 Las Vegas Blvd. S. (369–5222). *The Roaring 20s,* a rollicking tribute to the area.

Imperial Palace, 3535 Las Vegas Blvd. S. (794–3261). *Legends in Concert* —Janis Joplin, Elvis, Judy Garland, and others are re-created by impersonators.

Riviera, 2901 Las Vegas Blvd S. (734–5301). *Splash: An Acquacade Extravaganza,* recently proclaimed the Show of the Year in Las Vegas.

Sands, 3355 Las Vegas Blvd. S. (733–5453). *Sizzle,* dancers, singers, beautiful girls—the works.

DINNER THEATER

Union Plaza, 1 Main St., downtown (386–2444). Broadway comedies and musicals with name performers. Excellent dinner.

JAZZ

Four Queens Hotel, 202 E. Fremont St. (385–4011). *Jazz From Las Vegas,* every Monday night. Hosted by Alan Grant.

FEMALE IMPERSONATORS

Silver Slipper, 3100 Las Vegas Blvd. S. (734–1212). *Boy-Lesque* has been running forever and most people love it.

LOUNGE SHOWS

One of the big entertainment bargains in Las Vegas is the lounge show. All of the major hotels have entertainment in their lounges, starting from as early as 2 P.M. Usually, the only cost is the price of your drinks, and often there is not even a minimum. The lounge entertainers can be quite good, and often you will have the opportunity to see a star on the rise.

HOW TO SEE A SHOW

There are no actual tickets for most Las Vegas entertainment. What you do is call the hotel's show-reservation number on the day of the performance or the day before, tell them what show you want to see, and give them your name. Then, when you get to the theater, give the maître d' a nice tip ($5–$20, depending on the star quality of the performer) to assure yourself of a good seat, and he will call a captain to seat you.

Some time during the show, after your dinner or drinks, you will be presented with the bill, which you pay then. If the bill is for dinner, it will include the cost of the show. This can be a really good deal at the few hotels that still have dinner shows. Most of them are now just cock-tail shows, and their price includes a couple of drinks.

Shows in Las Vegas range from a low of about $5.95 a person to see something like "Boy-Lesque" (Silver Slipper) to a high of $50 to see Frank Sinatra. But the average is $25.

Show-room Seating

If you think that the show-room maître d' looks a little like an orchestra conductor, you're not far wrong. Few visitors realize that a good maître d' arranges his show room like the seating of an orchestra, with certain "instruments" here, others there—so that all will blend into a harmonious whole and create music that will make him and the hotel proud.

As you enter the show room, you may notice a sign on the other side of the rope that reads: "Invited Guests." And you may notice that the people arriving there do not need to stand in line. That's because they are high rollers, press, and assorted other VIPs.

The maître d' must make sure that these VIPs are seated in "king's row," which is the first tier of booths. He must fill all of those booths, but he also must make sure there is always one left for that "special someone" who may arrive unannounced or late.

The maître d' must then "dress" the room: good-looking, well-dressed persons who look like they will re-spond to the show, down in front; good tippers, wherever they want to be; slobs or drunks, to the rear; and a comped VIP, to the best seat in the house—de-pending on who did the comping. There are VIPs, and then there are *real* VIPs. The two most important hotel comps will come from the president of the hotel and the manager of the casino.

RONALD REAGAN IN LAS VEGAS

No wonder he has been such an entertaining president. He used to be a Las Vegas entertainer!

While President Reagan has not called attention to the fact, he once was a show-room performer in Las Vegas. The truth is, he made only one appearance in the Entertainment Capital of the World—on the stage of the Last Frontier (now the Frontier) Hotel in 1954—and since then, he has gone on to more amazing performances. Those who saw Reagan say that he was not all that bad, that he had a good sense of humor and a lot of energy.

No one remembers now how much money Reagan made, because compensation for Las Vegas performers can vary widely. When Liberace played the Last Frontier in 1947, he was paid only $1,500 a week. When Dolly Parton played the Riviera a couple of years ago, she was reportedly paid a whopping $350,000.

But that was the end of that. Dolly Parton's salary taught the Riviera and other hotels that there was a limit to how much you could pay a superstar and still make money. Today, star salaries range from a low of $50,000 a week to a high of $300,000. Julio Iglesias and Frank Sinatra are among the best paid.

Reagan could probably make more now than he did then. On the other hand . . .

COMPS

While you're standing in line waiting to get into a show, other people will waltz right past you up to the "invited guest line" and be ushered right in to a good seat. Who are they? you wonder. They are persons who have been put on the comp (complimentary) list because they lost a lot of money in the casino, they are press doing an article on or review of the show, they are friends of somebody important, etc. But when you get to the maître d', you can be treated just as well merely by showing him a little green from your wallet.

MOVIE THEATERS

Las Vegas has two very unusual movie theaters, and they are right across the street from each other. The **Omnimax Theater,** in Caesars Palace, is the world of the future. Inside a dome that you can see from the street, the theater offers a nearly wraparound screen, scores of thundering speakers, and films that have been especially made for the Omnimax process. The films last about 45 minutes, and they run them all day. Not to be missed. $3, adults; $2, children.

If the Omnimax Theater is the world of the future, the theater in the shopping arcade at Bally's is just the opposite. From the outside, the marquee looks like a 1930's neighborhood cinema. But the inside—ah, the inside is meant to resemble a Hollywood screening room, with soft, luxurious couches that seat only two. The theater was originally built by MGM when it owned the hotel (1973–86) and it showed mostly movies from the Golden Era of Hollywood, like *Casablanca, The Maltese Falcon,* and *Sons of the Desert.* Bally's liked the theater so much it decided to keep it. $3.50, adults; $2.50, children and seniors.

Another movie house, **Red Rock Theaters,** at 5201 W. Charleston Blvd., is mostly frequented by locals, but there's no reason why you can't go as well. Eleven movie theaters all under one roof, and most showing first-run films. $5.50.

BARS

Las Vegas is not noted for intimate cocktail lounges. Most of the places to drink here are either noisy lounges adjoining a casino, neighborhood beer bars, or singles bars. But there are a couple of places for a quiet drink.

REGULAR BARS

Huey's, 2600 E. Flamingo Rd. (732–8411). Large and attractive. Good Mexican food.

Mickey's, 1487 E. Flamingo Rd. next to the Clark County Library (737–0727). Quiet and intimate. Good appetizers.

Peppermill, 2985 Las Vegas Blvd. (735–7635). Opulence Las Vegas style: pastel wallpaper, plush sofas, waitresses in evening dresses, and a fireplace amidst it all.

Sandpiper, 3311 E. Flamingo Rd. (485–5555). A little further away but very nice. Has a piano player.

COCKTAIL LOUNGES

Arthur's, 4640 Paradise Rd. (737–0530). Nice place, popular with locals. Sometimes seems like a singles bar.

Botany's, 1700 E. Flamingo Rd. (737–6662). Brand-new, beautiful place. Also has an excellent restaurant. Favored by the Las Vegas cognoscenti. Sometimes looks like a high-class singles bar.

The Break, 2585 E. Flamingo Rd. (369–9598). Dancing nightly.

Cafe Michelle, 1350 E. Flamingo Rd. (732–8687). An authentic French sidewalk cafe and restaurant, but also an excellent place to go at night for a drink. Where the Las Vegas beautiful people go.

Cheers, 4110 S. Maryland Pkwy. (732–4474). Near

the university. Nothing like its TV namesake, but not bad.

Dispensary, 4912 S. Eastern, at Tropicana (458–6343). Attractive waitresses.

Omni Lounge, 6005 Las Vegas Blvd. S in the Hughes Terminal (739–1117). Watch the planes take off from Howard Hughes's old corporate headquarters.

Shenanigan's, 6145 W. Sahara Ave. (364–2535). Las Vegas's most modernistic gin joint, with long planes of plate glass, neon tubes, and steel beams.

Rube's, 4634 S. Maryland Pkwy. (736–7823). Across from the university. A nice, small place.

State Street, 2570 State St. (733–0225). Owned by Gianni Russo, who appeared in *The Godfather*. It's a high-class joint, the kind you could take yer mudder to.

COUNTRY-WESTERN BARS

Rockabilly, 4660 Boulder Hwy. (458–0096). A little out of the way but a nice place.

Sam's Town, 5111 Boulder Hwy. (456–7777). One of the most popular western dance places in town.

Silver Dollar, 2501 E. Charleston Blvd. (382–6981). A Las Vegas institution.

SINGLES BARS

Carlos Murphy's, 4770 S. Maryland Pkwy. (798–5541). Across from the university; attracts a student crowd; good Mexican food as well.

Chatters, 4801 S. Eastern Rd. (736–2711). A beautiful lounge with a piano bar. Popular with the Yuppie crowd.

Elephant Bar, 2797 S. Maryland Pkwy. (737–1586). Unusual decor; good drinks; not far from the Strip.

TGI Fridays, 1800 E. Flamingo Rd. (732–9905). Always crowded and lively; good drinks; not far from the Strip.

Tramps. 4405 W. Flamingo Rd. (871–1424) Voted

the most popular singles bar in Las Vegas by the readers of the *Review Journal.*

DISCOS

Krackers, 4885 E. Lake Mead Blvd. (452–6514). Rock 'n' roll; in North Las Vegas.

Mr. G's., 3105 E. Sahara Ave. (641–6666). Rockets and neon abound in this bizarre, outer-space nightclub, where all booths are in sawed-off chassis of vintage automobiles. Two dance floors; youngish crowd.

Packard's, 3824 Paradise Rd. (731–1050). Attracts a noisy young crowd.

DANCING

Alexis Park Hotel, 375 E. Harmon Ave., near Paradise Rd. and not far from Bally's Las Vegas (796–3300). This is the only major hotel in Las Vegas *without* a casino, and they planned it that way. The dancing is to contemporary music, overlooking the pool. A nice place.

Atrium Lounge, Tropicana Hotel, 3801 Las Vegas Blvd. S. (739–2222). One of the most beautiful dance settings in Las Vegas, and best of all, the music begins a little after noon.

Botany's, 1700 E. Flamingo Rd. (737–6662). The latest in place with the cognoscenti and beautiful people of Las Vegas. A DJ and contemporary recorded music.

Chateau Vegas, 565 E. Desert Inn Rd. (733–8282). Favored by an older crowd. Pleasant and quiet. Also has an excellent restaurant upstairs, Juliano's.

Las Vegas Hilton Lounge, 3000 Paradise Rd. (732–5111). The music, lively and loud, alternates with singers or comedy acts.

Mr. G's, 3105 E. Sahara (641–6666). One of the most popular dance places in town with the younger set.

Colorful and lively, with the most unusual architecture of any nightclub in Las Vegas. Live music and disco.

Omaha Lounge, Union Plaza, 1 Main St., downtown (386–2110). Live music in a variety of styles.

Palace Station, 2411 W. Sahara Ave. (367–2411). Live music with a variety of styles.

Skipper's Landing, 4563 E. Sunset Rd. (454–1887). A little out of the way, near Green Valley, this is the place to escape the tourist crunch and dance with a mob of desert locals of all ages.

Top o' the Dunes, Dunes Hotel (737–4110). A nice place to have dinner and a beautiful view of the most brightly lighted intersection of the Strip. Live music.

Top of the Landmark, Landmark Hotel (733–1110). A panoramic view of the city. Particulary favored by the romantic.

Top of the Mint, Mint Hotel, 100 E. Fremont St., downtown (387–MINT). Panoramic view of the downtown area. Closed on Monday and Tuesday.

NUDE SHOWS

Can-Can Room, 3155 Industrial Rd., behind the Stardust Hotel (737–1161). A more informal kind of place, with totally nude strippers but no alcoholic beverages. No cover charge, but they will charge you $7 just for a Coke.

Palomino, 1848 N. Las Vegas Blvd., North Las Vegas (642–2984). Mentioned on *The Tonight Show* by Johnny Carson. Well-produced striptease, the Las Vegas equivalent of The Crazy Horse in Paris. Completely nude. Cover charge, $7.50.

Pussycat, 4416 Paradise Rd. (733–8666). Seminude strippers, since the club is in Las Vegas, which does not allow total stripping where drinks are served. Cover charge, $7.50.

SEX FOR SALE

Nevada is the only place in the United States where prostitution in brothels is legal. It is *not* legal in Clark or Washoe counties, where Las Vegas and Reno, respectively, are located. It is legal, however, in Nye County (about 60 miles north of Las Vegas), where half a dozen brothels may be found.

Although prostitution is illegal in Las Vegas, at last police count, there were about 2,500 hookers working in the city. The number varies according to how many (and which!) conventions are in town, and there are more "working girls" around on weekends, naturally.

In addition, there are escort services that advertise in the local tabloid newspapers and seem to promise paradise on earth, though they can't legally promise you anything other than companionship. The city is trying to close them down.

Las Vegas also has become a magnet for what the police call the "weekend warrior": She may be a secretary in Phoenix or Los Angeles during the week, but on the weekend, she knows how to make a fast, tax-free $1,000 or more.

All of the above are to be avoided.

TEN THRIFTY THRILLS

Here are ten things you can do in Las Vegas that cost practically nothing. Further information about them may be found elsewhere in this book.

1) Omnimax Theater at Caesars Palace. A futuristic wraparound screen and scores of speakers. Movies especially made for this process. $2.50.

2) Hollywood-screening-room-style movie theater in Bally's Las Vegas. Classic movies from Hollywood's Golden Era. Adults, $3.50.

3) Circus acts performed all day and night on the mezzanine of the Circus Circus Hotel. Kids love it. Free.

4) Bugsy Siegel's Rose Garden, in the back of the Flamingo Hilton Hotel. A weird tribute to the "great man." Free

5) Elevator in the Mint Hotel to the Top of the Mint. Great view of the downtown area. Free.

6) Outside elevator at the Landmark Hotel. Another remarkable view of the city and the Strip. Free.

7) "Giant" shrimp cocktail at the Golden Gate Hotel, in the downtown area. Still only 50¢.

8) Complete T-bone steak dinner at the El Cortez Hotel, in the downtown area. Only $5.95, one of the great bargains of Las Vegas.

9) Have your picture taken—*free*—in front of $1 million in cold cash at Binion's Horseshoe, in the downtown area. Don't worry about all that money "not being used." Binion knows how to use it; he's been doing so for years.

10) Largest gold nugget in the world, on display—where else?—at the Golden Nugget, downtown.

Day Trips from Las Vegas

While Las Vegas is the Entertainment Capital of the World and a center for gambling, it also is the hub for some interesting excursions.

You would never know that from the air. Las Vegas is about equal distance (300 miles) from the two nearest cities, Los Angeles and Phoenix. When you fly into Las Vegas at night, it looks as if you are crossing hundreds of miles of black velvet before you reach the glittering jewel of Las Vegas. But that is only partially true. Here are some of the things you can see that are within driving distance of the city:

DEATH VALLEY

Death Valley is about 145 miles northwest of Las Vegas. Just take U.S. 95 north to State Highway 373. Turn left and follow the signs to Death Valley. There's a wonderful old inn there, the Furnace Creek Inn (mentioned elsewhere in this book), and a more modern motel complex. A word of warning though: Death Valley gets *very* hot during the summer; temperatures of 120 degrees are not uncommon. Be sure to pay attention to road signs that tell you what to do in case you have car trouble. The desert sun can be a killer, so it's much nicer to go there in the winter.

HOOVER OR BOULDER?

In 1985, Hoover Dam, just a short distance from Las Vegas, celebrated the 50th anniversary of its completion. At the time it was built, Hoover Dam was considered to be the greatest engineering wonder in the world.

You may be saying, "Wait a minute, don't you mean Boulder Dam?"

Yes, we *do* mean Boulder Dam, and we also mean *Hoover* Dam—and there's a story in that. It was always meant to be called Hoover Dam in honor of President Herbert Hoover, who was instrumental in the dam's planning.

But Hoover was no longer president when the dam was completed. Roosevelt was, and Herbert Hoover wasn't exactly the most popular man in town. Hoover's foes in Washington began calling it "Boulder Dam," derived from the Boulder Canyon Act of 1928, the law that authorized construction.

Then, to top it all off, President Roosevelt used the term "Boulder Dam" in his dedication speech there in 1935—and that was that.

In an effort to end the confusion, President Harry Truman asked Congress in 1947 to investigate and determine its real name. They did, and they found that it was "Hoover Dam."

But to this day, when you ask residents of Boulder City, which is next to the dam, how to get to Hoover Dam, most of them will answer; "You mean 'Boulder Dam,' don't you?"

Hoover Dam was created for two purposes: flood control and the generation of electrical energy. But the

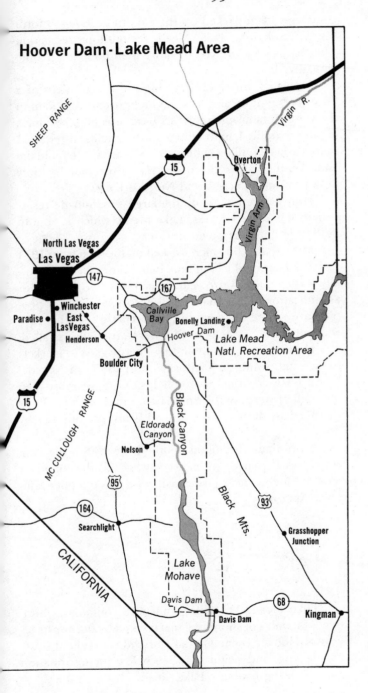

Hoover Dam - Lake Mead Area

completed dam backed up the Colorado River to form the 115-mile-long Lake Mead, an outdoor recreation area that is now enjoyed by more than 6 million people annually.

Hoover Dam is 727 feet high, the equivalent of a 70-story building, and it is the highest concrete dam in the western hemisphere. At its base, it is 660 feet thick, greater than the length of two football fields. It required more than 4.4 million cubic yards of concrete to build the dam, enough concrete to construct a two-lane highway between San Francisco and New York City.

Hoover Dam backs up the largest man-made reservoir in the United States, Lake Mead, which is able to hold 30 million acre-feet of water.

More than 5,000 men worked on the dam from 1931 to 1936. Despite the long time in building, the dam actually was completed two years ahead of schedule. And as an indication of the quality of the work, millions of people have visited the dam, but the terrazzo tiles that they walk on are the same ones that were originally installed.

Hoover Dam's nonpolluting energy goes to markets in Arizona, southern California, and southern Nevada. Water released from the dam helps to irrigate more than one million acres in the Southwest and in Mexico. Prior to the dam, farms were washed away periodically by floods.

More than 19 million people have visited the dam since it was opened. When asked what was the comment most frequently heard from visitors, a guide replied simply, "Amazing."

LAKE MEAD

Lake Mead, 115 miles long and containing more than 500 miles of shoreline, was created by the construction of Hoover Dam. The lake provides excellent boating, fishing, and swimming. See below for information about renting boats on Lake Mead.

THE VALLEY OF FIRE

The Valley of Fire is about 55 miles northeast of Las Vegas. Just take Lake Mead Boulevard east from North Las Vegas. The ride is a most attractive jaunt through the desert. The Valley of Fire is an open-air archaelogical "museum" of early Indian civilization in the area. The Indian petroglyphs (carvings on the rocks) are said to be as much as 50,000 years old. Free. For more information, call 397–2388.

LONDON BRIDGE

Who would have believed that some crazy American could buy up the broken-down old London Bridge, transport it stone by stone to the middle of the Arizona desert—and then make it a hit? That is exactly what happened here at Lake Havasu City, near the Colorado River in Arizona. Some say that financier Robert McCulloch thought he was buying the more famous London Tower Bridge, but no matter: London Bridge in Lake Havasu City is a glitzy and sweltering-hot tourist town, with a predictable Olde English Village alongside. The best place to stay is the new **Queens Bay Hotel,** overlooking the bridge. 1477 Queens Bay, Lake Havasu City, AZ 86403 (602–855–0888). London Bridge is 160 miles from Las Vegas. Go east and south on U.S. 93–95, turn left on I–80, and follow the signs.

ETHEL M CHOCOLATES

Ethel Mars was the woman responsible for the creation of the Mars bar. A couple of years ago, her son moved to Las Vegas and built a huge chocolate factory in Henderson. It makes Las Vegas' favorite chocolate (available in all the better hotels), including liquor-filled chocolates, which you are not supposed to take out of the state—but everyone does.

They have a beautiful factory, and they are the friendliest people around, as befits chocolate-makers. They offer a tour of their factory that is very popular, probably because they give you a free sample. The tour also includes a visit to their beautiful Botanical Garden and Cactus Display next to the plant. (Odd combination, chocolate and cactus.)

The factory is open 9:30 A.M.–4:30 P.M. daily, and self-guided tours are available at any time. The address is 2 Cactus Garden Dr., Henderson, Nev. 89015 (458-8864).

OLD NEVADA AND BONNIE SPRINGS RANCH

Visitors to Las Vegas who would like to learn what the Old West was like can do so by visiting Old Nevada and Bonnie Springs Ranch, which are only about 20 minutes from the center of the city. Just take Charleston Boulevard west.

Old Nevada is a replica of an Old West town, complete with live "shoot-outs," "hangings," and wooden sidewalks. In addition, the village is full of interesting shops and exhibits, for instance, the Sheriff's Jail, a museum showing the old clothes and other paraphernalia of the period. A manikin delivers a recorded message on the introduction of Nevada as a state.

The town is surrounded by some of the most attractive scenery in southern Nevada, so the ride out there is very pleasant. On the way, you will pass Red Rock Canyon, described elsewhere, so you can include that in part of your tour.

Open 10:30 A.M.–6 P.M. daily. $4.50, adults; $2.50, children; $3.50, senior citizens. Call 875-4191.

Right next to Old Nevada is the **Bonnie Springs Ranch,** which has a petting zoo for children and a horseback-riding stable. A ride through the desert can be a lot of fun when the weather is not too hot. The Bonnie Springs Ranch also serves up some fine food and drink, so you may want to plan to have lunch out there. Free.

MOUNT CHARLESTON

Mount Charleston, only about 30 miles northwest of Las Vegas, is a delightful contrast from the desert heat of the city. Because of its 7,000–10,000-foot elevation, the Mount Charleston area is at least 20 degrees cooler than Las Vegas, making it a wonderful destination for a picnic, for hiking, or for camping. The area is full of tall pines and mountains and lacks only a lake.

To get to Mount Charleston, go north on U.S. 95 to the Mount Charleston turnoff (about 10 miles) and turn left; you can't miss it. During the winter, a section of Mount Charleston—Lee Canyon—actually becomes a ski resort. Yes, skiing, just 30 miles from Las Vegas!

In addition, there's the Mount Charleston Lodge (386–6899)—with a huge fireplace in the center, where you can enjoy a drink or fine dining—and the new **Mount Charleston Hotel** (872–5500).

Hikers at Mount Charleston will find that in just a few short miles of walking, they can experience the climatic equivalent of going from central Mexico to Alaska. The best hike in the area is the Mount Charleston Peak trail, which goes right over the mountain, but it takes two days, since it is 16 miles long.

Other points of interest at Mount Charleston:

Angel Peak has radar domes on the summit. Visible from the Deer Creek Highway.

Cathedral Rock is a prominent rock with a spectacular view, located in the upper reaches of Kyle Canyon. Reached by a ¾-mile footpath.

Charleston Peak, at 11,918 feet, is the third highest peak in the state.

Deer Creek Recreation Area has a campground and picnic facilities.

Desert View Scenic Overlook, off Deer Creek Highway, provides a breathtaking view of the valley. Just a short hike from the highway.

Foxtail Snowplay Site, near Lee Canyon, has sledding and tubing, a popular area sport of sliding down snow-covered slopes on inflated truck-size inner tubes.

Kyle Canyon Recreation Area has two campgrounds and a large picnic area. Near the Mount Charleston Lodge.

Lee Canyon Recreation Area includes camping and picnicking sites, riding and hiking trails, and a winter ski resort with lifts, lodge, etc.

Mummy Mountain in silhouette looks like an Egyptian mummy.

Robbers Roost Cave is a limestone overhang that was once used by Mexican bandits as a hideout after their raids into Nevada and southern Utah. Accessible by a short trail from the Deer Creek Highway that goes between Kyle Canyon and Lee Canyon.

For more information on these Mount Charleston recreation areas and sites call 385–6255.

GRAND CANYON

While both the north and south rims of the Grand Canyon are about 300 miles from Las Vegas, that is considered to be a short distance in the West, so you might want to visit it while you are close by. It takes about 5–6 hours to drive there. (See *Tours* section for flights)

The Grand Canyon is the most spectacular natural wonder in the world. Stretching 277 miles along the Colorado River, it is the product of ten million years of erosion on Arizona's Coconino Plateau.

As the land has gradually risen, the great river has carved the Grand Canyon to a depth of almost a mile below the south rim and a width varying from 4 to 18 miles. Along the canyon walls, geologists have traced three of the five major chapters in the earth's history and have discovered rocks from the first geological era.

Although the Grand Canyon's recorded history began with its discovery by García López de Cárdenas in 1542, it has been the home of many ancient Indian tribes. More than 800 prehistoric living sites have been discovered within the canyon. Today, five major Indian tribes inhabit the area: Navajo, Hopi, Havasupai, Hualapai, and Paiute.

More than 60 species of mammals, 250 kinds of birds, 25 reptiles, and 5 amphibians live within the borders of the Grand Canyon.

Six of the world's seven climatic belts lie within the Grand Canyon. Its location makes it a natural year-round resort: high enough to escape the desert's heat in summer, yet far enough south to avoid the rigors of winter. Nights are cool, even in midsummer.

For hotel and lodge reservations at the Grand Canyon, call the Grand Canyon National Park Lodges reservations office (602–638–2401). There are also aerial tours of the Grand Canyon from Las Vegas.

RED ROCK CANYON

The most interesting scenic sight in the immediate Las Vegas area—which should not be missed—is Red Rock Canyon, just 15 miles west of the Strip. Only tour buses go there, so you will need to rent a car, but it is well worthwhile. Be sure to take your camera.

Just drive up to Charleston Boulevard, which crosses Las Vegas Boulevard (the Strip), and turn west. Eleven miles out, you'll see the sign to Red Rock Canyon Scenic Drive, a 13-mile loop, but you'll see the canyon well before you get there.

As the name implys, the sandstone walls are an

unusual shade of red, and their strange formations have been sculpted over the years by the desert wind. The visitor center there will explain how it all got to be that way.

If you are a hiker, you will find many interesting marked trails leading off the loop.

Colors on the Red Rock Escarpment can change dramatically, depending on the time of day. Sunrise and sunset are particularly colorful.

The scenic route is open 7 A.M.–8 P.M., Thursday through Monday. Recreational vehicles are allowed for day use only; there are no developed sites for overnight stays, but there are picnic areas.

For more information, call 875–4141.

BRYCE AND ZION CANYONS

As with the Grand Canyon, Bryce and Zion canyons are close enough to Las Vegas that you might wish to pay them a visit.

Visitors approach the rim of spectacular *Bryce Canyon* through a forest of ponderosa pine, spruce, fir, and aspen.

As you reach "The Pink Cliff" edge, a vast amphitheater comes into view: Freestanding spires, sculpted pinnacles, and multicolored minarets create a fantasyland for photographers and nature lovers.

The ever-changing effects of light on Bryce are spellbinding. Dawn and dusk, especially, produce visual effects that go far beyond one's imagination.

To get to Bryce Canyon, go north on I–15 to Cedar City, Utah for 180 miles, turn right at State 14, and then just follow the signs.

Unlike the ornamental spires of Bryce, *Zion Canyon* is massive and rugged. Stone steps lead to a half-mile trail that overlooks the canyon. The Virgin River courses through the park.

But Zion is not only a region of scenic beauty. A fascinating geological history is also evident here. At various times, the Zion area was covered by the sea, broad rivers flowed along its surfaces, or it was swept by desert winds. Today, its natural rock formations are awe-inspiring monuments to the effects of time.

One of the nation's oldest national parks, Zion has been described as a main canyon with several side canyons, carved from a high plateau by a river.

To get to Zion National Park from Las Vegas, go north on I–15 to St. George, Utah, turn right on State 15, and follow the signs.

Western-type cabins are available in both parks. For further information, contact TWA Services, Box TWA, Cedar City, Utah 84720 (801–586–7686).

NEARBY GHOST TOWNS

What would the American West be without ghost towns, those relics of a colorful past? Most visitors to Las Vegas are not even aware that there are interesting ghost towns in the area that you can visit. Nevada, the "Battle-Born State," was admitted to the Union during the Civil War because of the state's abundance of gold, silver, and minerals, which led to some of the state's colorful history.

It all started in southern Nevada. The state's earliest lode-mine activity took place at the Potosi Mine, near Las Vegas, which was initially worked in 1856.

Here is a selection of the most interesting ghost towns in the Las Vegas area. Don't plan to visit any of them if it looks like rain. Flash floods are always a possibility in the desert.

Potosi, on the old Spanish Trail, 25 miles south and west of Las Vegas and 4 miles from the paved road. There are mine and tramway ruins here you can explore. Just take I–15 south from the city and get off at exit 33 (Pahrump). On the road to Pahrump, at the top of the mountain pass, you'll see the sign indicating that the dirt road to Potosi goes off to the left.

(And if you're wondering about the name "Pahrump," it's the sound that Nevadans hear when marching to the beat of a different drummer.)

Goodsprings, 35 miles southwest of Las Vegas, is a colorful little mining town that still has a few inhabitants. Numerous old buildings and an abandoned railroad grade. Take I–15 south to the Jean exit, turn right, and you can't miss it.

Rhyolite, about 120 miles northwest of Las Vegas. Skeletal remains of two old banks, other buildings, and mines. Look for the old house made entirely of bottles (there wasn't much else to do when the mines petered out), and the colorful railroad station, which is still in pretty good condition. From a population of 8,000 in 1907, only six remain. Take U.S. 95 north and turn left at Beatty.

Sandy, 13 miles west of Goodsprings; just continue on the same road. Ghost town with a gold mill to sift the ore and a few abandoned mines.

Searchlight, 55 miles south of Las Vegas. Searchlight was a bustling mining center from 1902 to 1909. It rivaled Las Vegas at that time, but today, it is just a sleepy little town with few inhabitants. It's also a tourist stop on the way to Davis Dam, Cottonwood Cove, and London Bridge in Arizona. Take U.S. 95 east and south from Las Vegas.

TRAIN TRIP

If you have a little extra time and would like to take an interesting trip to Los Angeles, you can go there across the desert via Amtrak.

The Amtrak station is located in the back of the Union Plaza Hotel-Casino at 1 Main Street, downtown. In one direction lies Los Angeles, in the other Salt Lake City and points north and east. The train comes through once a day in each direction. Call 386–6896 or 800–872–7245 for the schedule.

A ride on the "Desert Wind" to Los Angeles is, in a way, a ride back into the past of the desert Southwest.

The train stations at Barstow—always one of the hottest places in the nation—and at San Bernardino look like Hollywood sets, and the Union Station in Los Angeles is a historical landmark. (There are also other stops along the way at Pomona and Pasadena.)

Amtrak says it has been "working on the railroad," and if the ride between Las Vegas and Los Angeles is any indication, it has. Its personnel are friendly and efficient, and the trains are clean. Don't expect too much for on-time operations, though. It is Amtrak, after all, not the TGV in France.

The food is no better than you might expect, but there is still something nice about sitting in the club car with a sandwich and a beer, watching the desert Southwest slip by.

Right across from the Union Station in Los Angeles is the colorful Olvera Street, an open-air Mexican marketplace and perhaps the single most interesting block in Los Angeles.

FIVE FUN ESCAPES

If the noise of slot machines and the nonstop action in Las Vegas become a little too much for you, if you want to get away for a while to something completely different yet nearby, then here are four suggestions:

HOUSEBOATING ON LAKE MEAD

Who has not fantasized about being captain of a ship? It's a fantasy that can come true. You can rent a houseboat for the weekend, and everything you'll need to know can be learned in a half hour before launch. If you can drive a car, you can drive a houseboat; it's that easy.

Lake Mead offers more than 500 miles of shoreline, with thousands of deserted coves where you can tie up for the night, grill some steaks on the houseboat barbe-cue, do a little skinny-dipping after dinner, and then lie on the roof and watch the stars for a while before retir-ing, lulled to sleep by the gentle rocking of the boat.

Living on a houseboat for a weekend on huge Lake Mead is as far removed from the glitter of Las Vegas as you can get. And it's only 30 miles away.

A houseboat, unlike a speedboat or a sailboat, prac-tically runs itself, so all you have to do is lean back at the helm and slowly enjoy life.

Most houseboats come in two sizes: a "six-sleeper" and a "ten-sleeper." Other than the inclusion of an addi-tional room, there is little difference in the boats. The ten-sleeper is 50 feet long; the six-sleeper, 36. But just because the boat sleeps six people doesn't mean that you *have* to take five friends. Why not just a cozy twosome?

All boats have a bathroom (real sailors call it a "head") with a shower and hot and cold water and a kitchen ("galley") with a refrigerator, pots and pans, dishes, silverware, and biodegradable soap.

The boats are also equipped with a gas-operated barbecue, air-conditioning, and even a stereo cassette deck! And they supply you with all of the bedding you will need, including blankets, since the lake can some-times get a little chilly at night. In reality, they are like floating motels.

The only things you have to bring are your own food, drink, a camera, and perhaps something to read and a deck of cards.

When you are ready to stop for the night, just run up into a friendly looking cove and secure the boat with the stakes that are provided. In the sleeping quarters are bunks, both double and single, but you certainly will want to lie on the roof for a while and look at the stars.

Starting a houseboat is merely a matter of turning on the ignition key after you have had the blower on for a while. In front of you is a lever, much like the shift in your car. When you want to go forward, you push the lever forward. When you want to back up, pull the lever back. It's as simple as that. For the rest, you just steer with the wheel.

FISHING

Fishing is excellent on Lake Mead. There are largemouth bass, striped bass, rainbow trout, cutthroat trout, and black crappie. The person who rents you the boat also can rent you fishing equipment and tell you how to get a three-day license.

Among the interesting places to visit—if you must have a destination in mind—is Hoover Dam. You can get pretty close to the dam.

While the boat companies do not recommend it, you can also pull into a quiet cove for the night and, with the aid of your cassette stereo, turn the houseboat into a floating disco just for the two of you. But if you're going to dance on the roof, don't drink; it's too dangerous.

Finally, houseboating has all the creature comforts of a fine motel, and all the romance of a cruise at sea on your own boat.

Rates for the rental of a houseboat for three nights, depending on the season, are: six-sleeper, $295–$615; ten-sleeper, $435–$850. Special rates for longer periods of time. For reservations or additional information call Callville Bay Resorts (702) 293–1904 or (800) 255–5561.

FURNACE CREEK INN

Rudolph Valentino would have loved this Death Valley hideaway, for the Furnace Creek Inn, about 145 miles northwest of Las Vegas, is a place where anyone can play the shiek.

Just walk out in the middle of the night to the labyrinthine pathway of the palm garden behind the sprawling inn. Stand at the edge of the stone wall and look out over that still, dark desert. The only sound you can hear is the wind rustling through the palm fronds.

The outside of the wall is so desolate that you could easily think you were the Son of the Shiek in your desert oasis. And an oasis is exactly what you are in.

The inn, a rambling affair the color of the desert, was constructed in the 1920s for the Pacific Coast Borax Company in the hope of bringing tourists to the desert. As everyone must know by now, Death Valley was once the home of *Twenty Mule Team Borax,* a radio show in which Ronald Reagan participated. But the borax industry was dwindling at that time, and tourism was seen as a possible way of saving the valley from economic disaster.

Death Valley was discovered by pioneers heading west. They nearly lost their lives there before they were able to get out, so it was named "Death Valley."

Temperatures during the summer can get as high as 134 degrees. Although the inn is air-conditioned, it closes around the middle of May because of the heat and reopens around the middle of October. The inn is owned by the Fred Harvey Corporation, which also owns similar properties in the national parks.

The inn opened for business in 1927 and is considered today to be one of the classic inns of America. Because of its proximity to Los Angeles, the inn has been used many times as a hideaway for movie stars; you may even see some while you are there.

The inn has a swimming pool, four tennis courts, a cocktail lounge, a supper club with nightly entertainment and dancing, an 18-hole golf course, and horseback riding through the desert at the ranch.

Since there are not many places to eat in Death Valley—two at the inn and two at the nearby Furnace Creek Ranch (a more modern motel complex that is open all year)—the inn operates on a modified American plan, which includes breakfast and dinner. Prices start at about $140 a day for a double. Prices at the ranch start at $35 a day, without meals.

Visitors will want to explore the Death Valley National Monument visitor center—which explains how Death Valley got to be that way (it was once a lake!)—and the Borax Museum at the ranch.

Tourists also should not miss a look at the Sand Dunes (14 miles from the Furnace Creek Inn), which were used in many Hollywood movies about the "Sahara," or a visit to Dante's Point, which overlooks the lowest point in America, Zabriskie Point.

Despite the geological wonders of Death Valley, you still may find that the real highlight of your trip was a stroll out to that mysterious and rustling palm garden behind the inn, where you stood at the wall with someone you loved and stared out at the forbidding desert . . . and thought of Rudolph Valentino.

For information on how to get to Death Valley, see the *General Information* chapter of this book. For reservations, call (619) 786–2345 or write Furnace Creek Inn, Death Valley, Calif. 92328.

MOUNT CHARLESTON

Las Vegans know a secret that many visitors do not know: If you want to get a little cooler during the dog days of summer, you drive up 7,000-foot Mount Charleston, which is only about 30 miles away.

It's hard to believe that in this desert there could be a mountain range with trees five feet thick and hundreds of feet tall, but that is the case. There is even a ski resort, Lee Canyon, up there.

Las Vegans have loved Mount Charleston, and with good reason. While a couple of hundred people live there, for the most part in rustic houses, the area has remained largely undeveloped, and that's the way they like it.

About the only commercial development has been

the creation of **Mount Charleston Lodge,** a charming ski resort that features a huge circular fireplace in the lounge and excellent food. Las Vegans and some visitors go there just for dinner. Despite the name, it has no rooms.

Some people have always felt that Mount Charleston ought to have a real inn so that people could spend the night without having to camp out. Now the area does, with the construction of **Mount Charleston Hotel.** Made of peeled logs and dark stone, it is beautifully in keeping with the nature of the area.

To get there, take U.S. 95 north from Las Vegas to the Mount Charleston cutoff, about 10 miles out. Then just follow that road to the inn.

The Mount Charleston Inn has 60 rooms and three suites, the latter with fireplaces. Rates are $49 for a room and $98 for a suite, Sunday through Thursday; $59 and $118, respectively, on Friday and Saturday.

For reservations or further information, call (702) 872–5500 or write Mount Charleston Inn, Kyle Canyon Road, Mount Charleston, Nev. 89124.

Mount Charleston is part of the Toiyabe National Forest, and there is ample opportunity there for camping, picnicking, and hiking. Just stop at the ranger station on Kyle Canyon Road for all information or write to the District Ranger, 1217 Bridger St., Las Vegas, Nev. 89101.

RAFTING THE COLORADO

The beautiful and wild Colorado River is so close to Las Vegas that you might want to consider rubber rafting while you are in the area.

A number of companies offer raft trips starting from Lee's Ferry, Arizona, that course the tamer sections of the river to the upper reaches of Lake Mead; others begin farther away, at Moab, Utah, but they put you into the wildest and most beautiful sections of the river—the parts you have seen pictures of in *Life* magazine and elsewhere.

Cataract Canyon on the Colorado provides some of the best white-knuckle rafting in America, and trips ranging all the way from two to six days are offered. Usually the raft holds ten persons, and the outfitters provide everything you will need, such as tents, sleeping bags, etc. The meals they provide on many of the trips are of gourmet caliber.

Since both Lee's Ferry and Moab are just little towns, transportation from Las Vegas is provided via aircraft. The cost of a trip ranges from $300 to $1000. It is definitely the thrill of a lifetime—but not for the faint-hearted.

Major companies offering rubber raft trips on the Colorado are

Moab, Utah: *North American River Expeditions,* 543 N. Main St. (801–259–5865); *Outlaw River Expeditions,* North Main St. (801–259–8241); *Tag-a-Long Tours,* 452 N. Main St. (800–453–3292); *Western River Expeditions,* 1371 N. Main St. (801–259–7019); *Wild & Scenic River Expeditions,* 293 S. 400 E. (801–259–8995); and *Wild Water Expeditions,* 543 N. Main St. (801–259–7838).

Lee's Ferry: *American River Touring Association,* 445 High St., Oakland, Calif. 94601 (415–465–9355); *Arizona Raft Adventures,* Box 697, Flagstaff, Ariz. 86002 (602–526–8200); *Colorado River & Trail Expeditions,* Box 7575, Salt Lake City, Utah 84107 (801–261–1789); and *Diamond River Adventures,* Box 1316, Page, Ariz. 86040 (602–645–8866).

Reno

Though it has neither the slickness of Atlantic City, nor the dazzle of Las Vegas, the "Biggest Little City in the World" has enough attractions of its own to draw some eight to ten million visitors yearly. The gambling palaces, of course, are the strongest tourist magnets. The allure of lucky keno tickets, million-dollar jackpots, and drawings for cars, gold coins, and dream vacations gives Reno's Casino Row an air of perpetual excitement. And if you want to party all night, the doors never close on your good times.

But 24-hour entertainment provides only part of the explanation for Reno's appeal. In a dramatic high desert setting sheltered by the rugged Sierra Nevada range, the city has more than its share of natural beauty. And the 115,000 people who live in Reno have an openness and *joie de vivre* that will put even the most cynical visitor at ease.

The town got its start in the 1860s as a toll crossing on the Truckee River, where ore from the fabulous Comstock Lode at Virginia City was brought down Geiger Grade by mule train. When the Central Pacific Railroad was routed through town in the latter part of the decade, Reno became one of the rowdier stations on the line.

It wasn't until the turn of the century that Reno gained notoriety as the "Divorce Capital of the World." Its reputation was well-deserved—tens of thousands of dollars' worth of discarded gold wedding bands have been dredged from the river in front of the County Court House. Reno acquired yet another "industry" when Nevada legalized gambling in 1931, but it wasn't until after World War II that casinos appeared on the large scale.

GETTING THERE

BY PLANE

Reno is served by 12 airlines—AirCal, American, American Eagle, America West, Continental, Delta, Eastern, Northwest, PSA, Skywest, Sunworld, and United—but since deregulation, the rundown changes with frustrating frequency.

Many of the casinos have complimentary shuttle service from the airport. Taxis cost $8–$9 to downtown hotels, $4–$6 to hotels in other areas. Limousine service is avialable, too, with $2.25 the going rate to downtown.

BY CAR

I–80 connects Reno to San Francisco, 225 miles to the west, and to Salt Lake City, 531 miles east. U.S. 395 is the north-south highway, linking Reno to cities in the Pacific Northwest and to Las Vegas, 441 miles southeast.

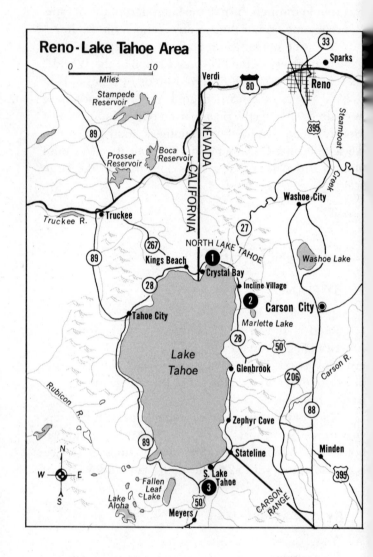

Major Hotel/Casinos

1) Tahoe Sands Resorts, Charmey Chalet Resort, Tahoe Vista
2) Club Tahoe, Incline Village
3) Caesar's Tahoe, Harrah's, Harvey's, High Sierra, Inn by the Lake, Station House Inn

BY TRAIN

The San Francisco-to-Reno Amtrak ride lasts about seven hours, and the trip through the Sierra Nevada is one of the most beautiful railroad routes in the country. The Salt Lake City-Reno train makes a all-night run of about 12 hours.

BY BUS

Both Greyhound and Trailways serve Reno and have stations within walking distance of downtown.

GETTING AROUND

You don't need a car to have a good time in Reno. Walking around the town a bit will allow you to see all the major tourist attractions, without the bother of parking. Those hotel/casinos in outlying areas—principally John Ascuaga's Nuggett, Bally's, and the Peppermill Hotel & Casino—can be easily reached by shuttle bus or taxi.

It's safe to walk down Virginia Street—Reno's Casino Row—at any hour, but stay away from the side streets after dark. Remeber that Reno has a very large transient population, and that not all of its visitors are law-abiding.

TAXICABS

Cabs in Reno are very inexpensive and there are plenty of them. It's a rare ride that costs more than $8.

BUSES

Citifair Bus Service can take you almost anywhere you want to go. The bus terminal, at 4th and Center streets, is spanking new. Bus stops are clearly marked. The fare is 60 cents for destinations within the city; you must have exact change.

RENTING A CAR

You can rent a car either at the airport or through your hotel after you arrive. Prices are comparable with those in other cities. The major companies are:

American International—395 E. Plumb Ln., 786–0184

Avis—Airport, 785–2727

Budget—444 N. Center St., 785–2545

Dollar—Airport, 348–7770

Hertz—Airport, 785–2756; Bally's, 785–2605; Harrah's, 788–3690

National—Airport, 785–2756

Thrifty—1893 Mill St., 329–0096

Remember that more than 90 percent of Reno's tourists come by car, which means a lot of drivers don't know exactly where they're going. The situation gets especially tricky after an overnight storm, when patches of black ice can be especially treacherous.

GUIDED TOURS

Two Reno-based companies provide bus tours of the area. *Reno-Tahoe Tours* (322–6343) offers eight-hour tours that include points of interest in Virginia City, Carson City, and Lake Tahoe in specially designed, 25-passenger buses. *Gray Line Scenic Tours of Reno and Lake Tahoe* (329–1147) features seven different tours May–October that depart from Reno in either 21- or 47-passenger buses. Helicopter tours are available, too.

CLIMATE

Due to its location on the eastern slope of the Sierra, Reno suffers dramatic weather changes. Despite these swings, the climate is generally sunny and dry. Though it snows, the snow usually melts in a day or two. Rains rarely last for more than a day. Temperatures from May through the first part of October are near perfect, in the 70–90° F range. Evenings are cool enough to allow a good night's sleep.

WHAT TO WEAR

Reno isn't the fashion capital of the world,—or even of Nevada, so don't worry a lot about what to wear. The emphasis is on casual, comfortable clothing; the only people you'll see in tuxedos are waiters. Jacket and tie are rarely required, but you may feel more appropriately dressed wearing them in the fancier restaurants. Be sure to pack both heavy and lightweight clothing if you come in spring or fall. Even summer, you'll often need a light wrap for evenings.

HOTELS AND MOTELS

Wherever you like to hang your hat—in a sumptious hotel suite, on a Victorian hatrack in a bed and breakfast, or on a willow branch in an RV park next to a rushing river—you'll find a place to your liking in the Reno area. The 20,000 rooms in the area range from country-western to Sodom and Gomorrah, with a lot of traditional decor in between.

Rooms are less expensive than you might expect. Suites cost $100–$500 and top-of-the-line rooms go for $80 and more during peak season (Memorial Day through September). In winter, however, many hotels slash prices drastically, offering rooms for $20 and less as well as bargain dining and entertainment packages.

Most of the hotel/motel accomodations are downtown. The major casinos away from the city center have shuttle service to downtown and are easily accessible by bus and taxi. The following selection will give you a head start on having fun. *Deluxe,* $70 a day and up; *Expensive,* $50–$70; *Moderate,* $30–$50; *Inexpensive,* under $30.

Harrah's Hotel/Casino, 219 N. Center St. (786-3232). Consistent high quality is the hallmark of this property. Rooms and food are among the best in town. The showroom features top entertainment, and cabaret revues are of Las Vegas caliber. *Deluxe*

The Wingfield House, 219 Court St. (348–0766). A grand old bed and breakfast with four antique-filled guest rooms. *Deluxe.*

Airport Plaza Hotel, 1981 Terminal Way (348-6370). Across from the airport, a good place to stay if you're combining business with pleasure. The hotel has a small casino, cheerful coffee shop, and fireplace suites. *Deluxe.*

Bally's Grand Hotel, Reno, 2500 E. 2d St. (789-2000). A hotel of superlatives, with the world's largest casino, a production show on the world's largest stage, two movie theaters, a 40-shop arcade, seven restaurants, 2,000 rooms (many with circular beds and mirrored ceilings), a 50-lane bowling alley, and an adjacent camperland for recreational vehicles. It's a must-see even if you stay somewhere else. *Deluxe.*

John Ascuaga's Nugget, 1100 Nugget Ave., Sparks (356–3300). The tasteful rooms are among the best values in the area. Facilities include nine restaurants, a showroom, and large casino. Lots of special events throughout the year. *Expensive.*

Holiday Inn Reno Downtown, 1000 E. Sixth St. (786–5151). Newly redecorated, with attractive rooms. *Expensive.*

Peppermill Hotel and Casino, 2707 S. Virginia St. (826–2121). The 16-story tower—Reno's newest—has luxury and penthouse suites on the top floor. The flashy casino is a favorite with the Friday double-your-paycheck crowd. Dining room, coffee shop, and buffet. *Expensive.*

Reno Hilton, 255 N. Sierra St. (322–1111). Popular with tour groups, the hotel also offers attractive packages to individuals. *Expensive.*

Daniels Motor Lodge, 4th and Sierra Sts. (321–1351). Two blocks from casinos, it's one of the more comfortable downtown motels. *Moderate.*

Eldorado Hotel & Casino, 345 N. Virginia St. (786–5700). With five restaurants, free entertainment on the casino stage, and the best exchange rate in town for Canadian tourists. *Moderate.*

La Quinta Inn, 4001 Market St. (348–6100). About three miles from downtown. *Moderate.*

The Vagabond Inn, 3131 S. Virginia St. (825–7134). Two miles from city center. With a play area and bunk-bedded rooms adjoining traditional guest rooms, it's ideal for families. *Moderate.*

Comstock Hotel & Casino, 200 W. 2d St. (328–1880). Western theme throughout, with the casino designed to look like a Gold Rush town. Good value. *Moderate.*

Circus Circus Hotel and Casino, 500 N. Sierra St. (329–0711). The place to stay downtown if you bring the kids. The exterior is pink and white striped, with a neon clown sign. On the mezzanine there's a full-scale midway, and circus acts are performed in the ring from noon until midnight. Rates are very low in winter. *Inexpensive.*

RESTAURANTS

With 350 restaurants listed in the yellow pages, Reno dining covers the whole range from gourmet dining in a sophisticated French restaurant to a hamburger in an eight-stool diner.

Here's a selective sampling of places to eat in Reno and nearby Sparks. For dinner: *Expensive,* more than $25 a person (exclusive of wine); *Moderate,* $15–$25; *Inexpensive,* under $15. For lunch: *Expensive,* more than $10; *Moderate* $5–$10; *Inexpensive,* under $5.

CASINO DINING

Le Moulin, Peppermill Hotel & Casino (826–2121). Excellent service and an extensive menu, with exotic specials like alligator, roe buck, and Arctic hare. *Expensive.*

Steak House, Harrah's Hotel/Casino (785–3232). Sophisticated ambience, with high-quality food and service. Try the broiled noisette of lamb, and be sure to save room for dessert. *Expensive.*

Top of the Hilton, Hilton Hotel/Casino (322–1111). On the 21st floor, with Continental cuisine and the best view in Reno. *Expensive.*

The Vintage, Eldorado Hotel/Casino (786–5700). Once inside, you'll forget you're in a casino. Over 300 choices on the wine list, some from owner Don Carano's California vineyards. *Moderate.*

Caruso's, Bally's Grand-Reno (789–2000). Though Cafe Gigi is the hotel's gourmet spot, Caruso's is a winner among the hotel restaurants for both food and prices. *Moderate.*

The Presidential Car, Harolds Club (329–0881). A $6.95 prime rib dinner, with lots of extras, is the specialty. *Moderate.*

John's Oyster Bar, John Ascuaga's Nugget, Sparks (356–3300). Delightful nautical decor, with John's Oyster Stew and Lobster Surprise Salad among the menu choices. *Inexpensive.*

BEST BETS AROUND TOWN

Ask Reno residents where they have fun dining, and you'll get a variety of answers. The following are among the more popular local choices for quality and value.

Bundox, 2 Lake St. (323–0324). On the banks of the Truckee River, with basic, well-presented Continental specialties. *Expensive.*

Leonardo's, 2450 S. Virginia St. (827–6200). Lots of tableside food and beverage preparation. The restaurant also houses the spectacular Caffee Vesuvio, which sparkles floor to ceiling. *Expensive.*

Bayern Stuberl, 595 Valley Rd., in the International Plaza (323–7646). European decor and lots of hearty German food give this restaurant a good helping of *Gemütlichkeit. Moderate.*

Colombo's, 145 W. Truckee River Ln. (786–5998). On an alley overlooking the river, with Italian specialties as fine as the views. *Moderate.*

Ichiban Japanese Steak House, 635 N. Sierra St. (323–5550). Teriyaki prepared before your eyes with a flourish of flashing knives. A moat-style sushi bar, too, with orders served via wooden boats. *Moderate.*

Rapscallion Seafood House & Bar, 1555 S. Wells Ave. (323–1211). Cajun-style blackened snapper and a great shrimp salad are among the stars on an all-star menu. *Moderate.*

Cafe 32, 8195 S. Virginia St. (853–3200). With art-deco decor, an outstanding choice for lunch. *Moderate.*

Liberty Belle Saloon & Restaurant, 4250 S. Virginia St. (825–1776). The place to go for delicious prime rib dinners in Gay-'90s surroundings. *Moderate.*

The Dragon, 1505 S. Virginia St. (329–6524). Great Chinese food and tanks filled with exotic fish are the recipe for a delightful evening. *Inexpensive.*

Miguel's, 1415 S. Virginia St. (322–2722). The best Mexican food in Reno, according to locals. *Inexpensive.*

BUFFETS

Though almost all of Reno's hotel/casinos feature all-you-can-eat buffets, they're not all created equal. You get what you pay for, and the following—all in the upper price range—are standouts:

Island Buffet, Peppermill Hotel & Casino (826–2121). Glittery, with waitresses dressed in sarongs. Best value is lunch, with great salad fixings and desserts. $5.50, lunch; $8.95, dinner; $12.95, Friday seafood dinner.

Skyway Buffet, Harrah's Hotel/Casino (785–3232). The lines are long, but it's worth the wait. The food is super and you won't have to eat breakfast next morning. $4.95, lunch; $7.95, dinner; $11.95, Friday seafood dinner.

Top of the Hilton, Reno Hilton (322–1111). Sunday buffet brunch is memorable, with everything from bagels and blintzes to eggs benedict and Belgian waffles. $8.95.

FAST FOOD, SNACKS AND PICNIC FARE

Cochon Volant, 1155 W. 4th St. (329–9977). Quick service, clever decor, and imaginative salads. *Inexpensive.*

Flakey Jake's, 693 N. McCarran Blvd., Sparks (359–4154). World-class hamburgers with extras like avocados at no extra charge. *Inexpensive.*

Guido's Pizza and Pasta, 1601 Vassar (322–7474). Bit-of-everything decor with billiard tables, arcade games, and good value for your dollar. *Inexpensive.*

Juicey's Giant Hamburgers, 301 S. Wells Ave. (322–2600). The cheeseburger with plank fries is top-notch. Other locations at 3280 S. Virginia and 104 E. Glendale, Sparks. *Inexpensive.*

Landrum's, 1300 S. Virginia St. (322–5464). A Reno legend, with eight stools, 24-hour service, and home-cooked meals like your mother made before she knew about cholesterol. *Inexpensive.*

Matterhorn Swiss Bakery, 612 W. 5th St. (329–6598). A gem of a bakery with irresistible Napoleons, Florentines, and sweet rolls. *Expensive* as far as bakeries go, but worth every penny.

Napa–Sonoma Grocery Company, Kietzke Lane and Grove (826–0595). Excellent picnic baskets make good use of fresh local produce. *Moderate.*

Semenza's, Neil Rd. and Peckham (825–4142). Super pizza and chicken wings. *Inexpensive.*

Tony's Delicatessen, 150 W. 1st St. (323–0521). Everyone buys Tony's sandwiches. *Inexpensive.*

NIGHTLIFE

After-dark excitement centers around—but does not end with—the casinos. Throughout the winter season, the Reno Philharmonic, Nevada Opera Guild, Reno Chamber Orchestra, and Nevada Festival Ballet perform. Music and dancing are of professional quality, since many of the performers earn their living in area showrooms and lounges. Now in its sixth decade, the Reno Little Theatre is the oldest of a number of theatrical groups.

Rock concerts, with groups like the Grateful Dead and the Moody Blues, take place at Lawlor Events Center, (784–4444) on the University of Nevada-Reno (UNR) campus.

On the casino scene, you might try:

Casino Lounge, John Ascuaga's Nugget, Sparks (356–3300). Drinks are exotic and there's a dance floor that's popular with local residents.

Circus–Circus Mezzanine, Circus-Circus Hotel/Casino (329–0711). Play midway games, eat cotton candy, and watch the circus acts.

Eddie's Fabulous 50's, 2d St. at N. Sierra (329–1950). The lounge has back seats of 1950s cars for booths and waitresses on roller skates in the restaurant.

Headliner Room, Harrah's, Reno (785–3232). The dinner show, with big-name entertainers, has the best showroom food in the area.

Hello, Hollywood, Hello, Bally's Grand (789–2000). Playing on the world's largest stage, this extravaganza, with its re-creation of the San Francisco earthquake, a waterfall cascading onto the stage, and other spectacular effects, is the one you shouldn't miss. *Tip:* Go for cocktails rather than dinner.

SHOPPING

Time was when Reno residents went to San Francisco for everything except toothpaste and tennis shoes. But not anymore. The Biggest Little City now has shopping centers and specialty shops galore, so you'll find plenty of places to have fun spending your money.

Eighty stores—including *Macy's* and *J. C. Penney*—are in **Meadowood Mall** (827–8450) at the intersection of S. Virginia St. and McCarran Blvd. The other large department stores, *Weinstock's* and *Sears,* are closer to downtown in **Park Lane Mall** (825–7878) at the intersection of S. Virginia St. and Plumb Ln.

Since you can find department stores all over the country, why not do some specialty-shop hopping? *Blue Banana,* at 267 Vassar St. (323–4831), is an outlet for hand-designed clothing and quality items made by area craftspeople. Some 600 species of tropical fish swim around in row upon row of aquaria at *Finarama* (329–1208) across the street.

At 1707 S. Wells Ave., *Dragon Springs,* (323–2298) intricate paper carvings, satin-robed puppets depicting characters from Chinese opera, and enamel earrings are among the hundreds of items produced in the People's Republic of China. *International Plaza,* 595 Valley Rd. (323–7646), carries magazines, tapes, dirndls, and gourmet German foods. At *Tokyo,* 3344 Kietzke Ln. (825–1533), cookbooks, fancy-design vegetable cutters, and other utensils are among the nonedible items for sale. If you're looking for chrysanthemum tea in pop-top cans, go to *Oriental Market,* 1095 S. Virginia St. (786–6122).

For a silver belt buckle or Western-style jewelry, try *Wade's Silver Shop,* 358 N. Virginia St. (329–9922), where you can also find bronze sculpture by leading western artists.*Parker's Western Clothing,* at 151 N. Sierra St. (323–4481), is a Nevada institution, with wood floors and antique showcases in which top-quality western hats, boots, and other clothing are displayed.

Earth Window, an Indian-owned shop in the **Indian Colony Shopping Center,** 2001 E. 2d St. (786–5999), is the place to go for high-quality cradleboards, moccasins, and Paiute Indian beadwork.

The work of 60 outstanding potters, most of them from Nevada, Northern California, and Oregon, is sold at *Feats of Clay* in the **Hillcrest Shopping Center** at 20 Hillcrest Dr. (826–1131).

Museum shops provide still more shopping options. If you're lookng for art books, unusual mobiles, or other creative items, go to the *Sierra Nevada Museum of Art* shop, 549 Court St. (329–3333). The shop at the *William F. Harrah Automobile Museum,* 970 Glendale Ave., Sparks (355–3500), is a treasure trove of auto-related books and memorabilia. There's a small shop at the *Wilbur D. May Museum* at Rancho San Rafael Park (785–5961).

Barnwood Is Beautiful, 135 N. Sierra St. (329–6106), features handcrafted picture frames of weathered wood made by Michael Pomerantz. The studios of award-winning weaver Kate Hanlon are located 20 minutes east of Reno at *Hardscrabble Farm,* just off I–80's Lockwood exit. In addition to shawls, jackets, and coats, you can buy Larry Hanlon's chess sets and custom furniture at the studio, but call ahead to be sure someone's there (342–0196).

Arlington Gardens, 606 W. Plumb Ln. (826–0337), is a charming clutch of boutiques in a former plant nursery. Miniatures, including an electric train setup with cars no more than a half inch high, fill a closet-size shop called *La Petite Maison.* Nearby, *Name Droppers* specializes in unusual stationery, gift wrap, invitations, and paper plates. *L'Agneau Handknits* features knitting-machine-crafted sweaters and made-to-order hand-knitted garments.

Don't forget the pawn shops, where many an unlucky gambler has left behind his or her disposables. Be advised that unless you're a darn good horse trader, you won't get any bargains. It's fun looking, though.

SPORTS

Seven golf courses, including the Lakeridge, designed by Robert Trent Jones; tennis courts; swimming pools throughout the city; and a number of fitness clubs mean you can stay in shape even if you are on vacation. The YMCA and YWCA welcome visitors, too.

If you want to take a hike, the Crooked Mile along the Truckee River at Idlewild Park and the path following the river in the downtown area make for walking with lots of great views along the way.

Spectator sports include baseball action with the Class A Reno Padres at Moana Field, UNR basketball games, and professional boxing matches.

SIGHTSEEING

Reno's non-neon attractions are an eclectic lot, ranging from a fledgling arboretum to one of the world's finest collections of antique vehicles. Here is a sampling:

Fleischmann Planetarium, northern edge of UNR campus (784–4811). A phenomenal fish-eye lens projector puts viewers in the center of the action as they explore the mysteries of outer space.

Great Basin Adventure, Rancho San Rafael Park (785–6133). Phase I of this children's amusement center opened in June 1987, with a re-creation of a mining stamp mill, a dinosaur sand pit, a farm with domestic animals, and a nature trail.

Harolds Club Gun Collection, Harolds Club (329–0881). Billed as the world's largest gun collection, it includes a revolver used by Jesse James and a pair of pistols Napoleon is supposed to have carried during his invasion of Russia.

Liberty Belle Slot Machines, Liberty Belle Saloon and Restaurant (825–1776). The world's first slot machine, invented by the restaurant owner's grandfather, is the centerpiece of this outstanding collection.

Nevada Historical Society Museum, 1650 N. Virginia St. (789–0190). Lots of local memorabilia.

Reno/Tahoe Gaming Academy, 133 N. Sierra St. (329–5665). Visitors learn to play twenty-one and craps, and are taken on behind-the-scenes tours of Club Cal Neva.

Sierra Nevada Museum of Art, 549 Court St. (329–3333). A small museum, with frequently changing exhibits of top artists' work.

Washoe County Library, 301 S. Center St. (785–4190). 1,300 living trees, plants, and shrubs grow inside.

Wilbur D. May Arboretum, Rancho San Rafael Park (785–5961). Only two years old, the arboretum is already one of Reno's beauty spots.

Wilbur D. May Museum, Rancho San Rafael Park (785–5961). Chronicles the department-store heir's travels around the world.

William F. Harrah Automobile Foundation, 970 Glendale Ave., Sparks (355–3500). The world's largest, the collection nonetheless is still one of the finest.

DAY TRIP: VIRGINIA CITY

In 1859, two Irishmen, Peter O'Riley and Patrick McLaughlin, discovered the Comstock Lode, the largest body of silver and gold ever found. Within months, a settlement of tents and frame buildings called Virginia City had become the world's most important mining center.

Crystal chandeliers, caviar, and champagne were the

order of the day in a town where men became millionaires overnight and miners earned a fabulous $4 per day. Furniture was imported from Europe. Sarah Bernhardt, Houdini, Lillian Russell, and Enrico Caruso performed at Piper's Opera House. And Virginia City gained international renown as "The Howling Wonder of the Western Hemisphere."

Today, Virginia City is a ghost town. Its 500 year-round inhabitants run souvenir shops and saloons on C St., with names like Bucket of Blood and Silver Queen. The atmosphere is Country-Western/Coney Island, with strains of cowboy tunes, jazz, and rockabilly wafting out of swinging doors.

Three early-day mansions—the Savage Mansion, the Mackay Mansion, and the Castle—are open for tours in summer. Piper's Opera House and the Chollar (pronounced "Collar") Mine are also open for visits. You can take a two-and-a-half-mile ride on railroad cars pulled by a steam engine from the historic Virginia and Truckee Railroad, or see the desk Mark Twain used when he was a reporter on the local *Territorial Enterprise*. St. Mary's in the Mountains Catholic Church has recently been renovated, and "The Way It Was," at the north end of C St., is an excellent museum that gives a vivid picture of Virginia City during the Gold Rush.

The town's big annual event is the Camel Races, held the weekend after Labor Day, when local personalities ride camels and ostriches along a course on D St. For more information call 847–0311.

Lake Tahoe

Mark Twain referred to it as "the fairest picture the whole earth affords." World travelers may feel that Twain was exaggerating a bit, but, almost without exception, they will admit that Lake Tahoe is among the most impressive alpine lakes they've ever seen. Walled in on all sides by stark mountains of pale granite, the lake is 22 miles long and 12 miles wide. It's one of the deepest lakes in the world, measuring 1,645 feet at its greatest depth, and containing enough water to cover the entire state of California to a depth of 14½ inches.

Dotting the shoreline are a number of towns, the largest of which are Stateline and Incline Village, Nevada, and South Lake Tahoe and Tahoe City, California.

GETTING THERE AND GETTING AROUND

Commerical flights land an hour's drive north at Reno-Cannon International Airport. Passengers bound for Tahoe can rent a car there or take the LTR bus ($12 one-way) to the south shore. The airports at South Lake and Truckee are used almost exclusively by private planes.

Most automobile travelers reach Lake Tahoe via I–80. California state routes 89 and 267 lead to the north shore; the south shore can be reached on U.S. 50 from Carson City to the east or Placerville, California, to the west.

Tahoe Area Regional Transport (TART) buses circle the lake on a regular schedule. During ski season, shuttle buses run from the casinos to the major resorts.

CLIMATE

At 6,225 feet above sea level, Lake Tahoe is usually a few degrees cooler than Reno. Annual average snowfall is more than 400 inches a year. Because of the altitude, it's a good idea to take it easy for your first day or two in the area.

WHAT TO WEAR

The accent is on informality at the lake. In summer you'll want trousers, shorts, and a bathing suit (for sunbathing; the lake is too chilly for most swimmers). Always bring a warm jacket, as the weather can get nippy even in July and August. Cocktail dresses, suits, and blazers are appropriate, but not mandatory, for celebrity show-rooms. Some of the fancier restaurants require jacket and tie.

HOTELS AND MOTELS

It would be going a bit far to say that Tahoe is lined with sleazy towns, but zealous newlyweds and newl-yunweds do tend to set the tone a bit. Still, the whole gamut of lodgings is available. Things tend to get a bit classier as you get closer to the towns of Incline Village and Stateline. Area code is 702 unless otherwise noted. The following are representative of the best Lake Tahoe has to offer. *Deluxe,* $90 and over; *Expensive,* $70–$90; *Moderate,* $50–$70; *Inexpensive,* under $50.

Caesar's Tahoe, Stateline (588–3515). Not quite as lavish as its Vegas counterpart, but you will find a sunken tub in your bedroom. *Deluxe.*

Harrah's/Tahoe, Stateline (588–6606). Among the country's most highly rated resorts, with sophisticated decor and TV and telephone in every bathroom. *Deluxe.*

Best Western Station House Inn, South Lake Tahoe (916–542–1102). Two blocks from the casinos, off highway, with a restaurant. *Expensive.*

Harvey's Resort Hotel, Stateline (588–2411). Mod-ern tower: large suites with picture windows offer mag-nificent lake and mountain views. *Expensive.*

High Sierra, Stateline (588–6211). Western theme, with costumed personnel. *Expensive.*

Hyatt Lake Tahoe, Incline Village (833–1111). On the northeast side of the lake. *Expensive.*

Tahoe Truckee Airport Inn, Hwy. 267, Truckee (916–587–4525). About 10 miles from the lake; lovely rooms. *Moderate.*

Pepper Tree Tahoe, 645 N. Lake Blvd., Tahoe City (916–583–3711). A block from the lake, newly redecorat-ed. *Inexpensive.*

Several real-estate offices specialize in condo and cabin rentals. Look for them in the yellow pages.

RESTAURANTS

All that mountain air is bound to make you hungry, and Tahoe is blessed with a number of very good restaurants. You can nibble your way around the lake at hamburger stands and pizza parlors or work up an appetite for a five-course dinner. Either way, you'll find that prices are reasonable: *Expensive,* more than $20 a person; *Moderate,* $10–$20; *Inexpensive,* under $10.

La Cheminée, 8504 N. Lake Blvd., Kings Beach (916 –546–4322). Intimate French dining room, with unusual regional specialties and hushed ambience. *Expensive.*

Le Petit Pier, 7252 N. Lake Blvd., Tahoe Vista (916– 546–4464). Tahoe's best and most popular French restaurant. Reservations a must. *Expensive.*

The Summit, Harrah's/Tahoe (588–6606). Splendid view of the lake and surrounding mountains, with elegant food and service. *Expensive.*

Chamber's Landing, Homewood (916–525–7262). Open only during the summer, with umbrella tables and a marvelous lakeside view. *Moderate.*

The Sage Room, Harvey's (588–2411). The oldest casino restaurant at Lake Tahoe, and one of the best. *Moderate.*

Stetson's, Del Webb's High Sierra (588–6211). Lots of mesquite-broiled dishes on the menu, lots of Stetson hats on the walls. *Moderate.*

Steven, 341 Ski Way, Incline Village (832–0222). On a mountain high above the lake, with spectacular views from the deck. *Moderate.*

Tahoe House, 625 W. Lake Blvd., Tahoe City (916– 583–1377). Swiss-themed, with a cozy atmosphere and alpine favorites like Schnitzel on the menu. *Moderate.*

J. Higby's Yogurt & Treat Shoppe, 591 Tahoe Keys Blvd., South Lake Tahoe (916–541–3034. Forty-two flavors of frozen yogurt and sundae cones that are showstoppers. *Inexpensive.*

Samurai, 3764 Lake Tahoe Blvd., South Lake Tahoe

(916–542–0300. Japanese fast food, with a first-rate sushi bar. *Inexpensive.*

PICNIC FARE

Since Lake Tahoe provides the ultimate in picnic spots, consider having some of your meals alfresco. Sand Harbor on the east shore and Kaspian Beach on the west are fun places to spread your picnic blanket.

The Gourmet Chalet, 521 N. Lake Blvd., Tahoe City (916–583–2292). Almost everything is homemade—quiches, salads, and an irresistible cheesecake.

The Cork and More, Boatworks Mall, Tahoe City (916–583–2675), and 1032A Tahoe Blvd., South Lake Tahoe (916–544–5253). Gourmet picnic baskets (24-hour advance notice required) include wine, Marcel et Henri paté, cheese, crackers, fresh fruit, and berry tarts.

NIGHTLIFE

When the sun goes down, the Stateline casinos light up with entertainment. The South Shore Room at Harrah's/Tahoe and Cascade Showroom at Caesars Tahoe showcase such show-biz personalities as Red Skelton, Julio Iglesias, and Dorothy Hammill, whose ice review comes to the lake each January. Newcomers on the way up and yesterday's stars perform in the casino lounges. For an August change of pace, you can watch Shakespeare under the stars at Sand Harbor on the east shore of the lake. Also popular during summer are the evening campfires at the state parks that border the lake.

SKIING IN THE TAHOE BASIN

The Lake Tahoe Basin boasts a large concentration of ski resorts, and their proximity to major towns makes it easy to combine action at the tables and on the slopes. Interchangeable lift passes allow skiers to sample several resorts in one trip.

Most of the 19 area resorts offer downhill skiing; several have both downhill and cross-country runs. During the season, you'll find races going on at one or more resorts each weekend. The most prestigious races, like the World Cup finals and celebrity challenges, generally take place at Heavenly or Squaw Valley. They're great fun for spectators, especially those with connections to get them access to the lavish spreads in the refreshment tents.

Here's a rundown of the major resorts:

Alpine Meadows, Squaw Valley (916–583–4232). With the longest season of the Tahoe resorts, Alpine covers 2,000 skiable acres with a base elevation of 7,000 feet.

Heavenly Valley, South Lake Tahoe (916–541–1330). The largest ski resort in the U.S., and also the closest to the casinos. Attracts affluent, big-city skiers. Five day-lodges, restaurants.

Kirkwood Meadows, 30 miles south of South Lake Tahoe (209–258–6000). Perhaps the most beautiful of the Sierra resorts, Kirkwood is surrounded by national forest and has the highest base elevation of all of them. Bars, restaurants, condo complexes, ski shops, general store.

Mount Rose, Mount Rose Hwy. (849–0704). A favorite with Renoites. Lodge, ski rentals and lessons, deli, cafeteria, bar.

Northstar-at-Tahoe, Hwy. 267 & Northstar Dr. (916–562–1010). Tall pine forests and aspen groves flank most of the runs. About half of the terrain is intermediate. A complete village with a variety of accommodations.

Royal Gorge, Soda Springs (916–426–3871). Largest cross-country ski resort in the country, and site of the 1986, 1987, and 1988 national championships. Has 62 trails and 255 km of machine-groomed track. Lodge, wilderness lodge, cafe, bar, shops.

Ski Incline, Incline Village (832–1177). Cafeteria, snack bar, cocktail lounge, lodging one mile away.

Squaw Valley U.S.A., Hwy 89, 8 miles of I–80 (916–583–6985). Site of the 1960 Winter Olympics, Squaw has 26 lifts—including a 150-passenger cable car. Restaurants, bars, shops, lodging for 2,000.

Sugar Bowl, off I–80 at Norden exit (916–426–3651). An older resort and one of the most charming, especially during the March Alpenfest, when an oom-pah band, German food, and costumed staff give it a European accent. Lodge, dining room, cafeteria, bars, video arcade.

SPORTS

Fisherman can either launch their own or rented boats, or go on sport-fishing expeditions on the Truckee River and a host of streams. Kokanee salmon, silver salmon, lahontan cutthroat, Yellowstone cutthroat, Kamloops trout, steelhead, rainbow, brook, and German brown trout are all caught in Tahoe's waters.

Several stables rent horses by the hour or the day. Guides are available and pack trips can be arranged. Thrity-two miles of bike paths follow the lake and there are opportunities for mountain-bike adventures. For hikers, the Tahoe Rim Trail offers spectacular views. Jeep, helicopter, and seaplane tours are available, too.

SHOPPING

Along with millions of tourists, many creative shop-keepers have discovered the area's charms, leaving no shortage of places to spend your casino winnings.

The arcade shops at **Caesars Tahoe** include *Gucci* and *Sierra Galleries.* Among the specialty shops at **Harrah's/Tahoe** are *Equinox,* for elegant clothes, and *Brittany Jewels International.* Outlets for *Olga* lingerie and *Hathaway* shirts are located in the new **Tahoe Keys Shopping Center** in South Lake Tahoe.

The Bavarian-style **Cobblestone Center,** on Tahoe City's main street, houses *Gundy of Scandinavia* and *Rauscher's Alpen Crafts,* with an emphasis on European imports. *Windy Moon,* in Tahoe City's **Roundhouse,** carries custom-designed quilts and quilt fabrics. Just across the way, *The Great Western Leather Co.* sells handcrafted bags, jackets, and halter tops. Specialty items at *Hemmings & Jarrett* include handsmocked girls' dresses. **Timberline** is Incline Village's shopping area, with gourmet kitchen items, wood collages, pottery, candles, and handmade jewelry.

SIGHTSEEING

While most people visit Lake Tahoe to catch the gambling glitter and enjoy its water/winter sports, sight-seers won't be disappointed. Here is a checklist of all attractions.

Pope-Baldwin Recreation Area. On the west side of the lake, north of South Lake Tahoe, a walking tour leads past restored Victorian summer homes of the wealthy.

Lake Tahoe Visitors Center. A nature trail with storyboards. At the Stream Profile Chamber you can view Taylor Creek at eye level.

Emerald Bay. The scenic crown jewel of Lake Tahoe, with gorgeous green water.

Vikingsholm Castle. Built in 1929, this 38-room replica of a Norse castle is considered one of the finest examples of Scandinavian architecture in the western U.S. A one-mile hike from the highway, it is open only in July and August.

The Ehrman Mansion. Sugar Pine Point State Park. The mansion houses a museum of early artifacts from the Tahoe Basin.

Fanny Bridge. Tahoe City. A great place to stretch your legs and watch the giant trout swimming in the water below. For a great adventure, rent a rubber raft at one of several places close by and drift down the Truckee River toward Alpine Meadows.

Ponderosa Ranch. Incline Village (831–0691). An amusement center with antique carriages, farm equipment, a wedding chapel, and a re-created western street of shops. The ranch's centerpiece is the legendary home of the Cartwright family of the "Bonanza" series on TV.

The M.S. Dixie (588–3508) and **Tahoe Queen** (916 –541–3364) take passengers on several daily cruises to Emerald Bay from the south shore of the lake. Party boats and sailboats, complete with crew, can be chartered.

DAY TRIP: CARSON CITY

Although it is no longer the smallest or quaintest of the American state capitals, Carson City stills draws attention for its cluster of picturesque 19th-century buildings in the center of town. With the help of a free map from the Chamber of Commerce on Carson Street, you can tour 28 of these architectural gems, mostly residences, whose styles range from "carpenter Gothic" to early Victorian. Among the more noted is the house of railroad exectutive Henry Yerington, with its solarium styled like a railroad parlor car. Nearby is the Nevada State Museum, which has been called one of the 10 best regional museums in the country.

The 50 stone buildings of the former Stewart Indian

School were recently placed in the National Register of Historic Places. The Prison Store at the Nevada State Penitentiary in town does a booming business in tooled leather belts, watercolors, hand-made clothing, and other merchandise fashioned by those currently doing time.

Carson City is 33 miles south of Reno and 25 miles east of Stateline in Lake Tahoe. For more information call 882–1565.

Index

LAS VEGAS (AND ENVIRONS)

FODOR'S TRAVEL GUIDES

Here is a complete list of Fodor's Travel Guides, available in current editions; most are also available in a British edition published by Hodder & Stoughton.

U.S. GUIDES

Alaska
American Cities (Great Travel Values)
Arizona including the Grand Canyon
Atlantic City & the New Jersey Shore
Boston
California
Cape Cod & the Islands of Martha's Vineyard & Nantucket
Carolinas & the Georgia Coast
Chesapeake
Chicago
Colorado
Dallas/Fort Worth
Disney World & the Orlando Area (Fun in)
Far West
Florida
Fort Worth (see Dallas)
Galveston (see Houston)
Georgia (see Carolinas)
Grand Canyon (see Arizona)
Greater Miami & the Gold Coast
Hawaii
Hawaii (Great Travel Values)
Houston & Galveston
I-10: California to Florida
I-55: Chicago to New Orleans
I-75: Michigan to Florida
I-80: San Francisco to New York
I-95: Maine to Miami
Jamestown (see Williamsburg)
Las Vegas including Reno & Lake Tahoe (Fun in)
Los Angeles & Nearby Attractions
Martha's Vineyard (see Cape Cod)
Maui (Fun in)
Nantucket (see Cape Cod)
New England
New Jersey (see Atlantic City)
New Mexico
New Orleans
New Orleans (Fun in)
New York City
New York City (Fun in)
New York State
Orlando (see Disney World)
Pacific North Coast
Philadelphia
Reno (see Las Vegas)
Rockies
San Diego & Nearby Attractions
San Francisco (Fun in)
San Francisco plus Marin County & the Wine Country
The South
Texas
U.S.A.
Virgin Islands (U.S. & British)

Virginia
Waikiki (Fun in)
Washington, D.C.
Williamsburg, Jamestown & Yorktown

FOREIGN GUIDES

Acapulco (see Mexico City)
Acapulco (Fun in)
Amsterdam
Australia, New Zealand & the South Pacific
Austria
The Bahamas
The Bahamas (Fun in)
Barbados (Fun in)
Beijing, Guangzhou & Shanghai
Belgium & Luxembourg
Bermuda
Brazil
Britain (Great Travel Values)
Canada
Canada (Great Travel Values)
Canada's Maritime Provinces plus Newfoundland & Labrador
Cancún, Cozumel, Mérida & the Yucatán
Caribbean
Caribbean (Great Travel Values)
Central America
Copenhagen (see Stockholm)
Cozumel (see Cancún)
Eastern Europe
Egypt
Europe
Europe (Budget)
France
France (Great Travel Values)
Germany: East & West
Germany (Great Travel Values)
Great Britain
Greece
Guangzhou (see Beijing)
Helsinki (see Stockholm)
Holland
Hong Kong & Macau
Hungary
India, Nepal & Sri Lanka
Ireland
Israel
Italy
Italy (Great Travel Values)
Jamaica (Fun in)
Japan
Japan (Great Travel Values)
Jordan & the Holy Land
Kenya
Korea
Labrador (see Canada's Maritime Provinces)
Lisbon
Loire Valley
London

London (Fun in)
London (Great Travel Values)
Luxembourg (see Belgium)
Macau (see Hong Kong)
Madrid
Mazatlan (see Mexico's Baja)
Mexico
Mexico (Great Travel Values)
Mexico City & Acapulco
Mexico's Baja & Puerto Vallarta, Mazatlan, Manzanillo, Copper Canyon
Montreal (Fun in)
Munich
Nepal (see India)
New Zealand
Newfoundland (see Canada's Maritime Provinces)
1936 . . . on the Continent
North Africa
Oslo (see Stockholm)
Paris
Paris (Fun in)
People's Republic of China
Portugal
Province of Quebec
Puerto Vallarta (see Mexico's Baja)
Reykjavik (see Stockholm)
Rio (Fun in)
The Riviera (Fun on)
Rome
St. Martin/St. Maarten (Fun in)
Scandinavia
Scotland
Shanghai (see Beijing)
Singapore
South America
South Pacific
Southeast Asia
Soviet Union
Spain
Spain (Great Travel Values)
Sri Lanka (see India)
Stockholm, Copenhagen, Oslo, Helsinki & Reykjavik
Sweden
Switzerland
Sydney
Tokyo
Toronto
Turkey
Vienna
Yucatán (see Cancún)
Yugoslavia

SPECIAL-INTEREST GUIDES

Bed & Breakfast Guide: North America
Royalty Watching
Selected Hotels of Europe
Selected Resorts and Hotels of the U.S.
Ski Resorts of North America
Views to Dine by around the World

AVAILABLE AT YOUR LOCAL BOOKSTORE OR WRITE TO FODOR'S TRAVEL PUBLICATIONS, INC., 201 EAST 50th STREET, NEW YORK, NY 10022.